PETER BONAKER

SACRED
SHIELD

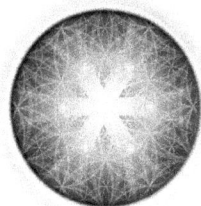

Shamanic Protection for
the World Today

GRATITUDE

To all who have suffered the maladies of Mordrigal and found the love within themselves and their hearts and reached deep within to realize their own self-love! Hats off and bravo!

To all of my teachers starting with the Great Spirit and then including all whom along the way on this great soul's journey have been my teachers, mentors, and guides.

DEDICATION

COVID-19 and the opportunities deeply embedded offering us the choice to walk in freedom, as terrifying a proposition as that may be.

THANK YOU

To Dan the Word Man, Maureen the Book Whisperer, Kristen and John for getting it, and the love and encouragement, most of all, from my clients, students, friends, and family. Thank you!

CONTENTS

INTRODUCTION

THE WAYS OF
THE EARTH

Love is something you and I must have. We must have it because our spirit feeds upon it. We must have it because without it we become weak and faint. Without love our self-esteem weakens. Without it our courage fails. Without love we can no longer look out confidently at the world. We turn inward and begin to feed upon our own personalities, and little by little we destroy ourselves.

With it we are creative. With it we march tirelessly. With it, and with it alone, we are able to sacrifice for others.

Chief Dan George
in Kent Nerburn. *The Wisdom of the Native Americans.*

It is an arduous task to write about something that dances on the dark side. It is impossible to be all things to all people, yet the importance of the task at hand cannot be understated. This book is about an energetic form that is very elusive in nature. It is an energetic form that I refer to as *Mordrigal*. Other writers over the past 100 years have referred to this dark energy by naming it and each describing its vagrancies as a most malevolent energy that attacks individuals' souls with a vengeance, even being cannibalistic in nature.

It appears that most books in the new-age genre of writing have one noticeable absence of information. That absence is a warning that very real reasons to proceed with a certain degree of awareness and caution also exist. It is not simply about "butterflies and rainbows" as one of my client's favorite sayings went. Not all energies are perfectly peaceful and benevolent. There are energetic forms that are just waiting for the opportunity to enter one's field, given certain conditions and circumstances. *Sacred Shield* delineates some of the situations where one may be quite vulnerable to being "hit" in a manner of speaking. This book portrays a route to a healed condition, should an individual, an acquaintance or a loved one be experiencing conditions similar to any of the situations described herein. This writing ideally provides and promotes an awareness that could enlighten us all as we proceed through the turbulent times of the 21st century.

This book is the culmination of being consumed with a sense of responsibility and urgency to bring forth a specific body of information that has emerged for me over fifteen years as a shamanic practitioner. My background includes an extreme trauma and near-death experience at the age of sixteen. I worked for thirty years as an educator at all levels in public education, from pre-kindergarten through to the twelfth grade. Following that, I taught post-graduate students as an adjunct professor at the University of Denver for ten years and also, oddly enough, worked as a licensed building contractor (still to this day). Simultaneously during this last period, I began my studies and teaching in the field of shamanic healing.

Along the way on the shamanic part of this journey, I became curious about how a certain number of people repeatedly presented the exact same definite pattern reflecting the presence of what I came to know and describe as a very dark energetic form. The pattern never deviated and is quite unusual in contrast to the standard teachings in the shamanic field. This dark energetic form knows no boundaries of any kind that can be consistently determined. In the shamanic field, I have had the opportunity to work with individuals throughout the entire world. There appear to be no economic, geographical, ethnic, gender, or other types of borders or boundaries that this dark energetic form refused to cross. Any and all individuals appear to be equally available, particularly when they might happen to be especially vulnerable for one reason or another. Many aspects of information briefly presented here will further unfold throughout this book.

It is important to clarify where the information written about in this book originates from. Beginning my training in 2005, through to the current times, every client session has been documented (appendix A and appendix B), over 1,350 client sessions in total. Well more than 500 of those sessions have dealt specifically with the same dark energetic form and its non-deviating projection on the chakra systems.

An analysis of the data between the years of 2008 and 2016 was completed in the fall of 2016 by an independent data analyst. The analysis from these years provides an approximation about the prevalence of this specific energetic form within my shamanic practice. The early years prior to 2008 were eliminated as mostly attributed to the learning curve in developing my shamanic skill and practice. The years following 2016 leaned toward higher numbers in that clients came for healing sessions based on referrals from teaching

The summary statement presented below reflects the gross numbers of the data analysis from 2008-2016.

CLIENTS 2008 – 2016 (8 YEARS):

36/189 total client base = 19% of Total Clients Experiencing the Same Energetic Expression*

291/860 total session = 34% of Total Client Sessions Dealing with the Same Energetic Expression*

*(appendix A: blank one-page data collection form; appendix B: sample completed data collection form)

When adding in the gross numbers through the year 2018 of clients suffering from the energetic form, the percentage of total clients increased to 29%. The numbers for the percentage of total healing sessions dealing with the dark energy increased to 47%, nearly one-half of all treatment sessions. Again, the added numbers become much less predictable in that the leaning is toward more referrals due to greater awareness of the intervention strategy and protocol presented within this book. Add the data for additional years since then, and these percentages only increase, almost exponentially.

Just by definition alone, also consider that this group of clients is initially sorted by their seeking the services of a shamanic practitioner. We know that the general public may tend to consider shamanic intervention as alternative and rare as a health care option. What is important here is understanding that this data is the basis of the information from whence this book was written.

Many questions have persisted over time. What is the dark force? How long has it existed? How long do you think I have had it? Can I get rid of it? And so on. The answers rest within the pages of this book to the degree that they are known.

In many instances, it is only descriptions or manifestations that will have to suffice to answer the deepest questions. Throughout this writing, stories of clients and their journey to a healed state will be described and interpreted. The process here is the OUTING of this energetic form. The nature of this energy is that it is elusive, non-descript in nature, and therefore lends itself well to its victims being described as psychologically disturbed. It also lends itself to much the same kind of description for a writer, practitioner, and teacher who would dare bring this information forward.

There is a progression in presenting the information. First and foremost is answering the question of what are shamanic protections, and why are they important? I have a friend who is a 90-year-old Catholic priest, and when we talk about most aspects of this story, he will usually say, "I have no idea what you're talking about." Hence, that is the most immediate challenge.

Once there is some basic understanding of why protection is important, the concept of the Song of the Soul is introduced. The Song of the Soul is a rhythm, a hum, or a vibration that comes with an individual as they enter into their world of existence. That rhythm stays with an individual as a constant that will never go away. The Song of the Soul is a place where a sense of self and satisfaction with who we are exists. It is a metaphor, yet quite real in the respect that it reflects contentment and a feeling of rightness. When one hears or experiences their Song of the Soul, they know they are home. The story around the dark energetic form described here, on the other hand, is all about the interruption and hijacking of the Song of the Soul.

Next will be an initial attempt at defining shamanism and the world of the shamanic practitioner, followed by a chapter introducing the dark energetic form in-depth, that of the energy of Mordrigal.

Chapter 5 is entitled "Soul Fractures," which may be the main point of this work. The concept of soul fracture is about the deepest traumas in one's life and where these traumas are held from an energetic perspective. This is most important as soul fractures can be resistant to healing through traditional therapeutic approaches, such as talk therapy. Further, I hypothesize that these fractures are the openings where the dark, malevolent forces find entry into one's energetic body. The field for delivering therapeutic services may be able to benefit from a broader and deeper penetration into ways of viewing and understanding the soul. Healing at that level carries the potentiality to provide unprecedented results less typically found in traditional models of service delivery.

Chapter 6, "A Turn to Healing," shares some very deep examples of how isolation plays into the long game for this dark energetic form. Following this, another very important aspect of this work provides an in-depth rendering of the protocol for the removal of this energy.

Lastly, the final chapter wraps up with "The Empowerment of the Soul." The essence of Sacred Shield is the dynamic of healing for all who may be afflicted with the deep, malevolent energies of Mordrigal. The hope rests with the love mentioned in the opening. A clear understanding that it is not to love the energetic form, but rather to love oneself, is the greatest deterrent of this energy. Doing one's work and working from the heart is the greatest protection. It is when we nurture ourselves in any manner at all that this dark energy finds it to be intolerable. This energetic form will often begin to lose interest in its victims when they are caring for themselves. In medical terms, Mordrigal is the bacteria, and the Sacred Shield is the penicillin. It is hearing and knowing the Song of the Soul, being connected to one's higher self.

Regarding the practitioner, these teachings launch one into broadening their intervention strategies overall, again within all levels of client work. With respect to the client, these understandings broaden one's approach to and understanding of the long-term aspects of these treatments. These are the shamanic protections for our world today.

......

Oh, the comfort, the inexpressible comfort of feeling safe with a person, having neither to weigh thought, not measure words, but pouring them all right out, just as they are, chaff and grain together, certain that a faithful hand will take and sift them, keep what is worth keeping, and with a breath of kindness, blow the rest away.

Dinah Maria Craik, *A Life for a Life*

......

CHAPTER 1

SACRED SHIELD: WHY DO WE NEED PROTECTION?

I t has become evident that there is an urgent need to bring a dark energetic form to the light. This means bringing certain aspects of our frame of thinking from unawareness to that of being brilliantly aware of it. There can be inherent dangers when dark energies have free rein. It is an important time to find hope within ourselves and together as a greater community. It is probable that dark energetic forms may be acting in a manner that is similar to a malignant cancer growing within many of us, if not all of us.

I would like to share a story about a client who came to me in very difficult circumstances.

This client represents a position where, in the over 500 documented healing sessions dealing with the energetic form named Mordrigal, his rapid healing took place within the context of one session. It turns out that the phenomena of managing this energy in one session have been rare, though not without some other examples of managing this energetic form in short order. Regarding the overall treatment history of working with the Mordrigal energy, it has been more typical for any number of sessions to be required. DP, short for Data Point, the pseudonym I have given him, provides a relatively excellent starting point in describing why an individual might want to seek out the services of a trained shamanic practitioner. Throughout the remainder of this book, all case examples are presented with pseudonyms to protect their identities and confidentiality.

DP had just returned from an international trip to South America whereupon his return, he was physically ill, proceeded to urgent care, and followed that with an emergency room visit to one of the local hospitals. DP had been having suicidal thoughts over the previous two weeks prior to contacting me for an individual healing session. Most importantly, he also reported that he was not sleeping, which is a circumstance that intensifies any condition one might describe. Working with a specific protocol and removing the energy he had attracted, he again found his way back to the feeling of being himself, to hearing his Song of the Soul. We were able to divert the process of becoming isolated from himself, his family, his friends, and his soul. Herein are some details from my notes of his telling the story.

Prior to leaving on a long-planned international trip to South America with his wife, DP had mild symptoms of being sick. When he arrived, his symptoms became progressively more intense. DP referred to his stamina as "soldiering on" to keep with his commitment to staying the distance for this long-planned vacation. While in the last city on their tour, things took a turn for the worse. In a park across from their hotel, where music and dance seemed to be the order of the day, they enjoyed their time there. The entrance to the park was opposite a row of buildings that caught his attention. His curiosity grew until he began to notice one particular building that gave him a type of chill, a dark feeling inside, and one that suggested he would do best to avoid this building at all costs. Ironically, on the last day of their vacation, a walking tour ended by going into that very building for a visit. The building was the "Inquisition Museum." DP's description:

> As I proceeded through the museum, my mind was telling me of the thousands of souls that had been tortured. It was like you didn't have a remote

control so you could change the channel. You were
in it. As we departed the museum, my health was
getting incrementally worse. Over the past several
days, I had been working out a way to get back
to the States. There had been a strike, so as the
airlines resumed, it would have been a very long
return trip. I ended up just purchasing another set
of tickets to get home. Again, I was getting sicker
by the moment.

Back in the States, they went immediately to an urgent care
center at their first landing point. He received some medicine
that helped his situation stay under control. However, upon
finishing the medicine, DP describes something hitting him
in a more than devastating way. As his health deteriorated
further, he also began to feel symptoms, such as shame and
even thoughts of suicide. He was reminded of a similar state
of being some eleven years earlier, that lasted for several
months. He shared that he was not about to endure the kind
of isolation he had experienced at that time. Thus, he began
reaching out to do everything he could to deter the feelings
he was having. This included many traditional strategies
accepted in Western medicine. After thoroughly exhausting
all avenues available and still being in a desperate situation,
DP reached out to request a shamanic healing session. He felt
it was predestined in that we knew each other, he had some
idea of the type of work I engage in as a shamanic practitioner,
and that I was available to him on an immediate basis. The
night prior to DP contacting me, he was at one of the local
hospital emergency rooms where he was being assessed for his
suicidal ideation. The hallmark of the entity is isolation, and

for DP, a pattern of vignettes of very dark ideas of how he was going to kill himself were in play. Again in his words:

> By 1:30 am that night, they did a whole battery of tests and couldn't find anything wrong. They gave me a sedative. Then, also they did a psychological evaluation, wheeled in some type of monitor to assess my mental state and a Psychiatrist entered who asked if I was still wanting to kill myself. I knew that if I said yes they would keep me for three days. So I said no. Not really so much at that time. The day after the hospital, I have some type of a pill that allowed me to get a few hours of sleep. That would help to begin taking the pain away.

> At that point, I had met all of my obligations and fulfilled all of the things I had promised I would do. Then I picked up the phone and called. I said "I'm having thoughts of suicide" and he said I can see you in an hour. I had a session and recognized that I had an entity that he was an expert on.

> I had a shamanic session and it wasn't off-putting. I found it almost familiar, even though I had never done it before. There was a very subtle shift. It wasn't like you go into a hot-tub or you put your head in a freezer. It was an energy shift you wouldn't notice if you weren't paying attention. I was also alert to what was happening. I almost see myself there now. I can replay the whole thing, that close, that attentive. Afterwards, the metaphor I can come up with is it's like driving a car and what was going

on, looking in the rearview mirror, is now behind
you. It was very short lived, in the context of what
happened over 4-5 months 11 years ago.

I share this story because DP represents an acute dynamic that
could be dealt with rapidly and because he was not interested
in going through an episode he had experienced previously.
DP demonstrates that with the right lens and with rather
immediate attention, an individual can mediate this out very
quickly. However, what may be unusual is that his time lag
was very short between his being inundated and receiving
the multitudes of interventions he sought out so rapidly. It is
about the Song of the Soul, and DP began hearing his song at
that moment of intervention.

This is not to say or judge anyone else, as through the data
collected, treatment is typically longer, sometimes much
longer. The fundamental criteria here is that of building
bridges back to one's life as they know it and understanding
that this Mordrigal energy likes very much to disturb that
knowingness of the life systems, the hearing and experiencing
of the Song of the Soul. The longer this energetic form has
purchase within one's soul body, the more challenging it
becomes to remove it.

For some unexplainable reason, ultimately in its worst, most
devastating form, this energy as a dark force wants people to
kill themselves, to commit suicide. However, there are many
degrees of involvement with Mordrigal. It is nearly impossible
to determine an exacting list of reasons and causes for the
infiltration of the dark energetic form onto and into individuals'
psyches. It is easy to only think of the most severe scenarios for

individuals affected, yet there are as many levels of involvement as there are individuals impacted. Therefore, there are also numerous levels regarding the process of healing. The energy of Mordrigal, which is the name I have selected for this particular dark energetic form, is insidious at best. This energetic form is clever yet wholly non-creative in its presentation. The most disturbing aspect of this energetic form is that it seemingly has access, once infiltrated within the individual, to that person's subconscious as its personal library to use in terrorizing the specific victim it has opportunistically invaded.

Another way to understand the Mordrigal energetic form would be to consider how a newly identified form of the influenza virus is found every year. Mordrigal is similar. Some peoples' fields are more porous than others. It is highly variable as to who gets hit, how hard, and what it may take for each person to heal. Issues such as car accidents, unexpected traumas, childhood traumas, and forms of PTSD can all create a splinter or tear in the inner fabric of their soul. The entry of the dark, unwelcome energetic form then overrides the natural protections. It is then that the individual needs a Sacred Shield to restore their natural shield, their natural protections.

Should an individual have a tear in their field, Mordrigal attacks because there is vulnerability. A solution may rest with the Sacred Shield. Living in a toxic world, an individual can be opened up to parasites. The Mordrigal energy is quite similar to a parasite. It attaches and sucks the life out of its victims. The use of awareness-altering items such as alcohol, marijuana, ayahuasca, and other substances can increase one's vulnerability to the opportunistic invasion of energies like those of Mordrigal.

Regarding this energy, it is a matter of maintaining a high

vibration. Good energetic protections begin with a kind of energetic hygiene. This is caring for what is taken into your body, into your mind, and most importantly, what is taken into your spirit. Superstition has little value in the world of energetic hygiene. It is practices of healthy food intake, healthy information intake, and most importantly, mindfulness of all of the relationships that surround us.

Regarding the situation for DP, he went to vignettes suggesting that he take his life. How could this be? Somehow this energetic form infiltrated his psyche to such a degree that some kind of inner dialogue was stimulated that had to be related to an imprint he holds deep within. I specifically have no idea what imprint was activated, only that it was this energetic form that had taken over his moment-to-moment living.

This degree of unwelcome energetic invasion has presented itself repeatedly in over 500 specific energetic healing sessions, as noted within the database from which this writing is taking place. Thinking of DP's experience, the attack was intense, pointedly when his resistance was low or non-existent. In his case, we had a friendship over the past several years, and he was aware of some of the work I had been involved with, if only peripherally. DP had some sense that I held an awareness of the dark energetic form he might be experiencing and shared with me that he knew all along that he needed to make contact with me. It was necessary for him to exercise all intervention avenues prior to contacting me to satisfy the traditional and typical viewpoint for those experiencing such conditions. It was necessary for him to bring his wife along in his treatment process. Exhausting the traditional medical intervention model was necessary prior to his contact with me. It is not unusual that a client who comes to a shaman for healing work will have expired all other interventions before considering that there may be something else involved with their situation.

One of the commonalities found within this massive gathering of data over the past fifteen years is that those suffering to the greatest degree from this energetic form are individuals who have experienced some degree of extreme trauma within their life's spectrum. Within this writing effort, there is an entire chapter titled "Soul Fractures." This term is referring to the experience for many of these clients where a severe trauma has occurred during their lifetime.

In particular, severe trauma related to abuse at one level or another is where the energetic form of Mordrigal finds its foothold within the psychic makeup of the individual. It is the trauma in its unrevealed state that leaves an opening to invasion by this dark energetic form of Mordrigal. This invasion then ignites the dangerous inner dialogues (shame), which manifest outwardly in all sorts of negative ways. Those negative manifestations are not always in ways that can be seen and treated by standard practitioners. This notion then lends itself well to the idea that it is the shamanic practitioner that can best identify and extract this energy, beginning the deeper healing required. I suggest here that it is the trained shaman with the tools in place to extract this level of severe energetic attack that is best qualified to intervene effectively with this most devastating, unwelcome energy.

Severe trauma places the individual on a continuum of unworthiness, loss of self-worth, self-confidence, and sometimes a loss of self-identity. This energetic form, once finding its foothold within an individual, binds into their language, most often their inner dialogue. Nearly impossible to determine where that is, the interventions proposed in this book fundamentally work for the client by removing this energy from them. Once that happens, the client can then experience their "self" without the dark energetic form. It is a process of bringing this separation between the individual's true self and the infiltrated self to the surface of consciousness. It is a matter of understanding the difference between being unknown to known, internal to external, and realizing the difference between what the energetic form is as well as the individual's true self. As the client grows in that awareness, they begin the process of separation, which then allows for the necessary deep healing of the original trauma to take place without the interference of the Mordrigal energy.

This is a summary of what this book is about: identifying, extracting, separating, and healing. There are many degrees of involvement ranging from a situation like that of DP in the example above to individuals who may suffer throughout the duration of their life. It is a matter of shining the light of consciousness on 1) identifying the signature footprint, 2) removing the energetic form, 3) experiencing the difference between having it and not having it, and 4) realizing the remedy of the deeper healing.

Sleep loss, nightmares, and even some types of tics—in the worst scenarios—can be in full expression. The individual is literally neurologically disheveled, where something is happening in their body that they may not be able to control. This energetic form can integrate itself into the autonomic nervous system. One client consistently asked me to work on her right big toe that was hurting her severely. The doctors, unable to find anything, kept telling her there was virtually nothing wrong with that toe. I started working on her right big toe because that's how this energy was manifesting. The dark and unwelcome energies being referred to manifest in different ways by accessing each individual's unique library of subconscious and unconscious experiences. There was another client who had pain right above her left breast, again with no diagnosable basis to it other than it was this energy manifesting in some type of Achilles' heel for that individual. What reason? It doesn't matter, as that was how it was manifesting for that individual. Pressures in the jaw, the temple, or the tongue starting to make clicking sounds were each a symptom that represented indicators to the trained eye that there was an energetic form present within the individual.

When a person is violated as a young person, they are naive and relatively unaware in their perspective because they are still in development. They do not know that their experience is not how the world is. The young person is unaware in their understanding that all children were not experiencing the same level of violation as what happened to them. There is normalcy that they expect from that treatment, and that then only grows for them. As they go into adulthood, sometimes with the memories of the violations being totally blocked from memory, the true trauma of that experience arrives. One client shared that she was forty years old when she realized that she had been abused as a child. She did not understand until then that she was treated in ways that other people were not treated. The early experiences of trauma then live in individuals' lives, carrying a wound that causes them to be vulnerable in a way that is different from the vulnerability someone who has not experienced such treatment. This is exactly where an energetic form like the one described enters the individual's soul body.

First and foremost, this book ideally brings forth hope and the idea that there are ways for one to walk in their world with protection. We are often led to seeing a very flowery or flamboyant type of perspective when we look into the unseen energetic world. There are, however, dangers in this realm that we are sometimes unaware of and not prepared to deal with. These forces can have extraordinarily negative impacts on one's life, particularly when there is a certain degree of naivety present. Yet, experience in the amazing world of energy can also be most extraordinarily exhilarating and expanding, especially when one experiences the "dark night of the soul" and successfully journeys through to the other side where the "bright light of the soul" also resides.

Shamanism is the oldest form of spirituality. Shamanism has existed in indigenous cultures around the globe for thousands of years. They are the medicine women and men of every community, able to operate in the invisible realm. They are the liaison, the ambassador, between the esoteric realm of energy and the earth that we live on. There is rightfully a process of celebrating the positive energies that emerge when an individual seeks out their highest soul's journey. *Sacred Shield* is written with an eye to protecting people against intrusions where unwelcome energetic forms may be present. Yet, some energetic forms may present as an interruption of purpose, interruption to the soul's journey in this lifetime. From this point forward, even reading this book and beginning to increase this understanding, the reader, and perhaps someone near and dear to them, is taking a first step to reclaiming life, independence, and sovereignty from the type of negative energetic forms described here. Reality is that we walk in a world of energy. There are energies all around us, all the time, every minute of every day, in everything we do.

Speaking to this phenomenon, it may be helpful to create a larger context within which to hold this information overall. There is a historical perspective that may facilitate a deeper understanding and openness to the nature of the discussion around the Mordrigal energetic form. I would like to introduce three authors with similar knowledge and experience regarding dark energy, similar to the Mordrigal energetic form described herein.

One author, dating back 100 years, addressed the same fundamental phenomena presented here. Her work is worth considering. In the 1920s, a writer named Simone Weil wrote extensively about the concept of affliction (*The Simone Weil Reader*, edited by George Panichas, 1977). Upon discovery of her work, it was stunning to realize a nearly exact description of what has emerged in the body of work described here. It appears this dark energetic form may have expanded since that time, or perhaps we are just becoming more aware. These specific dark energies may have always been here, as there are indications that it goes back many hundreds of years. It may, in fact, be emerging onto the surface in greater magnitude and could be playing a significant role in ways greater than we imagine. We tend to be living in times where less and less common agreement exists within our cultures and larger social groups. These kinds of divides may be creating an opening or tear that is similar to that of the hypothesized tear or rip in the individual's fabric of their soul. Where this tear exists, the dark energetic forms can then enter the individual and perhaps even have play at the larger social level.

Jack Forbe's, in his book *Columbus and Other Cannibals* (1992), described this energetic form as being cannibalistic and then referred to it as wetiko. That is the name referenced back through the many generations of our indigenous brothers and sisters. Paul Levy, in his book *Dispelling Wetiko* (2013), furthered Jack Forbe's work by naming the same force as *malignant egophrenia*. No matter, this energetic form has existed in all societies for time eternity. Perhaps what is different from 1920 to 2020 is that this energetic form has surfaced now at greater levels than ever, becoming more pervasive, invasive, and prevalent. These authors will be addressed with more depth in the discussions in chapter 5 around soul fractures.

This Mordrigal energy is opportunistic. Trauma has emerged, in this body of work, in that the unhealed traumas, the unhealed experiences that cross a certain boundary, open up the door, the seam in their being for this extremely dark energy to enter and take over. Severe trauma like being abused, being physically knocked around, or verbally shamed while growing up creates fertile ground and openings for this malevolent energetic form to take hold of its prey. An individual may not even know they carry the potential because they have spent their whole life in being shamed to one degree or another. These are the people who this energy hits, and this energy loves. This energetic form is an opportunistic entity that seizes on anyone with vulnerability, and perhaps, something as basic as being in the wrong place at the wrong time.

CHAPTER 2

THE SONG OF THE SOUL

Ev'ry soul hath its song, its melody divine
Every soul hath its song, its melody devine
Rising to extasy: and so hath mine.
Every soul hath its song, its melody divine!
Just let me sing my song, My song devine,
Let me sing, let me sing, let me sing my song devine:
Ah let me sing my song devine,
Let me sing my song devine,
Let me sing my song divine
Or I shall die . . . of sorrow.

"Song of the Soul." words by Edward Locke, music by Joseph Carl Breil. Featured in Universal's Movietone Production *The CLIMAX*.

S ound is used in the world of energy because of its frequencies and harmonies. Sound can be used as a very powerful tool to soothe, protect, or extract energies within. When we are talking about the Song of the Soul, we are also talking about the power of sound and the energetic world. The natural world is a major part of the energetic world. Shamans pull information from the natural world.

There are frequencies of sound that we are hearing, though we are not always consciously aware when that is happening. Our pets—dogs, for instance—will alert us when there is a frequency that's not right, that's not correct. Cats will go running and hide in the closet because they are hearing a frequency that we are not hearing, and they are getting that it is not the right one. It's not the one they were expecting to hear.

Science has proven there are many sounds, frequencies, and harmonies that are beyond the human capacity to hear, but they are measurable and quantifiable through the use of scientific tools. While theoretical and/or metaphorical in the esoteric sense, the Song of the Soul does exist. It exists in real time. Just because you cannot hear it in your ear, you know it exists in your heart. You know that you are hearing the Song of the Soul when you feel happy, peaceful, joyous, loving, compassionate, connected, inspired, creative, and hopeful. Those are all coming from the Song of the Soul. They are in your essence. Emotions are the lyrics of the Song of the Soul. Thus, if the Song of the Soul is flowing and singing its tune well, your emotions are peaceful, harmonious, loving, compassionate, inspired.

Dr. Emoto's work on the water molecules in his book *The Hidden Messages in Water* (2004), brings forth the astounding perspective and discovery that water molecules respond to music and to words. The most beautiful formations come when love and compassion are communicated, while hostile words and sounds present chaos and much less formed molecules. These may well be Songs of the Soul manifested in water molecules, which comprise very large percentages of whom we are as human beings manifested in physical bodies. We begin at close to 100 percent water in the womb and decrease as we age to nearly 50 percent water by the time we reach our 80s or 90s.

Inquiring within the sound healing field, practitioners, developers, and manufacturers all attest to the notion that each individual's vibration is the determining factor as to what notes have an effect. In other words, each person has their own unique Song of the Soul. When thinking about the healing aspects of sound, the role of intention emerges as of utmost importance. Sound, combined with the intention set by the healer, very likely plays the most important role in healing. In fact, intention is quite significant to all healing endeavors, no matter the principle format for the healing. However, just as important is the intention of the client. I have often sat back and wondered, *Is it not the belief, the intention set by the client, that they believe the healing will work and then it will?* Conversely, if the client does not believe this field of endeavor is viable, then the healing will not work. I feel as though I have seen this in action throughout all of my years as an energetic field healer.

If one cannot hear the Song of the Soul, then the Song of the Soul has been interrupted, hijacked, or interfered with. The Song has not gone away. When lyrics appear, the language that binds within the individual's inner dialogue are the words of the Mordrigal energetic form. These lyrics are hijacking or interrupting the Song in such a way that they eventually become contentious, angry, and vile. When these types of lyrics begin to appear, it can be a clue that there is an energetic force at play. The Song of the Soul is part of the validity of this writing. The Song of the Soul is a metaphor, yet it is real in the considered essence of the luminous energetic field that we all have surrounding us.

It is the Song of the Soul within the energetic field that every person—and perhaps every living thing on Earth—carries and supports throughout their lifetime. The Song of the Soul is a metaphor for the experience of being connected to our higher self, our soul self, our bright light of existence. The

Song of the Soul is where the soul's story comes from, lives on, and then transports forward to future times. It could very easily also be described as the place where the DNA, the ancestral inheritance, comes from and is held. There is always a Song that is yours. We just have to locate our songs. Another concept for the Song of the Soul may be your "light of the soul," or light energy.

Crystal Tones in Salt Lake City, Utah, which is one outlet for items such as singing crystal bowls, suggests that one's chakras all resonate differently depending on their levels of physical, emotional, mental, and spiritual development. Again, each one of us has our own unique Song of the Soul, our own unique experience of our rhythm, tone, and melody. Healing with sound, among other modalities, will always be unique to the individual and their level of development, on whatever scale one may wish to measure and intervene on.

Every sentient being experiences a Song of the Soul. Animals have a Song of the Soul, just the same as your trees have a Song of the Soul. Clemens Arvay writes about the *Biophilia Effect* (2015, translated 2018) that research has been able to determine that terpenes are given off by trees. These terpenes communicate with our autoimmune systems. We have no idea when this is happening because we absorb and experience the communication through our skin and lungs. Japan has an entire field of medicine referred to as forest bathing, traditionally known as Shinrin-Yoku. When an individual gets themselves into the environment of the forest, things start happening. One may feel better. It is the communication between an individual's body system and what the energy from the trees are telling you. The communication is occurring.

There is a sound frequency that we don't know we're hearing, but we are hearing—or perhaps better put, we are feeling and experiencing. These communications reside deep within us as they are communication with our most basic nature, as we are home when we are in the forest. It is our most basic nature. Studies have been completed that document the lowering of cancer cell numbers by sitting on a tree stump, as odd as that may sound to the uninitiated.

Amos Clifford, in *Your Guide to Forest Bathing* (2018), writes how our forests and trees need us now more than ever and that we have a need for the healing the forest has to offer. However, we have mostly forgotten how to be in our forests. In fact, we have so completely forgotten that the larger community is decimating our forests, wiping them out at an ever-alarming rate. It is an unintended consequence where, ultimately, we are harming ourselves. These are communications in sound that we are essentially unaware of, yet the soul experiences these energies, whether they are melodies, wordless tones, rhythms, and hums—or simply aromas, terpenes, or others.

Everyone and everything has a living essence on this planet. If they did not have a Song of the Soul, how is it we grieve so dearly at the loss of a pet or the loss of a tree? It is because their song is not in our lives anymore. I recall having a large maple tree die in my backyard and being so aggrieved and feeling guilty because I felt I had caused it to die by leaving all sorts of building materials around the base of it, smothering its source of life. I have found myself in the position of assisting friends and colleagues with the transition of the soul of their dog or cat when they have passed on. This assistance is because their grief was so profound at the loss of the Song of the Soul of their favorite pet, a member of their family. Their song stops playing with the Song of the Soul of the individual and of the family. It has stopped dancing with us! It is the harmony and the frequency that has been lost; the melody, that song is no longer there. He or she never spoke, though it was this kind of little wordless music. It was the rhythm that was carried with them.

Then there are rocks, which can hold an entire energetic field. They hold a lineage within them. Rocks are the record keepers of all time, and they tell stories of millions of years. They tell us about our history as a planet. The rock formations tell us how we evolved.

Most crystals that are found in the ground have very fine lines. Those fine lines are information lines. I carry a cloth wrap, which is the medicine bag of the tradition that I work in. Inside the mestana cloth are thirteen rocks by any name, yet when empowered through ceremony, these rocks become powerful carriers of the lineage of the tradition—the indigenous shamans of Peru and the historic Sun Empire. Once the mestana is opened, the brilliance of the lineage springs forth, and the healing work becomes guided through the lineage. The work becomes much greater than the individual healer by herself or himself. The work is guided by the lineage. The rock does carry its own rhythm.

It is particularly important to hear the Song of the Soul since it is one's ultimate protection. It is the ultimate shield because if a person is constantly hearing his or her own harmonies and frequencies of their soul, they always know who they are at their highest level of perfection. Their highest self is present.

This is our first and best definition of the Sacred Shield. The Song of the Soul existed before we were on this planet and will exist when we end our time here. Our emotions are the expression—the voice, if you will—of the Song of the Soul. When those emotions express joy, compassion, and love, then we know we are in harmony with your Song of the Soul. We will be operating as our highest self and in our highest peak potential of energetic expression, our ideal. That is the Sacred Shield.

It may be a matter of progression where if we start not hearing the Song of the Soul, listening less and less, then a distracted, noisy world can increase the potential for a malevolent energetic form to enter. This energetic form still finds its entry point through a trauma portal—a soul fracture, so to speak. When and if this happens, our ability to hear the Song of the Soul greatly decreases. At that point, one can completely lose the sense of remembering his or her highest spiritual essence or higher self. This is where the power to heal resides. When we hear our own Song of the Soul, then our ability to also hear the collective Song of the Soul greatly increases. It is possible that when an interruption takes place to our own Song of the Soul, then some type of meta-cognition is also absent. We become disconnected from our frequency, and then we cannot hear others' frequencies either.

When a person is born, he or she comes into this world with their own harmonies, their own frequency. Those frequencies are connected to their soul and sing away throughout the entirety of one's life. It is the wordless combination of harmonies. The individual's essence throughout their human lifetime, which they will always hear or experience on some level, is the internal rhythm that is their Song of the Soul. When a person hears the Song of the Soul, they know they are home.

Constant and unwavering, it is always available to the individual who is hearing and experiencing it even in their subconscious. The Song of the Soul cannot be altered, turned off, or damaged. It is constant. It exists within the individual. It is intertwined with the essence of who a person is. It is the harmony and frequency of their own soul. It is like a fingerprint harmony. It's unique only to the individual. When hearing one's Song of the Soul, they feel the essence of being in ayni, a Qechua word describing the right relationship with the world around an individual, being at peace with one's self.

This song does not have a dialogue. Every human being, no matter their culture or background, receives their song. The song does not have worldly limitations. It does not have language limitations because it comes with the soul. The Song of the Soul comes with all the information from past lives and ancestral experiences. These points of information always come in whatever language was playing for the soul, so it is not words. It is a rhythm, a melody.

There is evidence of technologies that existed in the very distant past that may have allowed certain things to happen, which we no longer have information about today. We do not understand the power that exists in sound. In travel to Peru, one of the great examples of this seemingly lost technology exists when visiting Machu Picchu and Cusco, the heart center of the former Sun Empire. There are walls and buildings where enormous blocks, presumably weighing many tons, are perfectly set with one another, stacked upon one another in perfect harmony. This building happened well before the invasion of the conquistadors in the 1500s.

Another example might be St. Peter's Cathedral in Rome, built during the renaissance period. How was this accomplished? There is marble tile perfectly round up to six feet in diameter set with brass or copper grout lines, with the next piece of marble perfectly set against the circumference of the circular tile piece. Today this would be nearly impossible, stated from the perspective of having set thousands of square feet of tile myself. There may exist skilled craftsmen today who could accomplish such a creation. However, it would be quite rare. Some people have said, "Oh, it was probably just built on the backs of slaves." It may do us well to consider the existence of previous societies prior to our recorded histories (as in eons of time). It appears to be almost incomprehensible that technologies could have been sophisticated and, in certain ways, superior to some of the technologies in our own time. The sophisticated use of sound may be one likely candidate for auditory technologies lost.

Think now of the role church bells played in everyday life in the past. Some European villages can still hear the church bells with stunning frequency. One might be reminded when we chance upon singing bowls or crystal bowls how harmonic attunement can be achieved.

The world of sound is enormously important. A dear associate and friend is a sound healer who sings an entire healing. The true ayahuascaderos who have trained for years in conducting the now-famous ayahuasca ceremonies, transmit their healing through sound, whistling, and singing to nurture the healing powers of the mother plant. Within the Peruvian culture, this is universal, having little to do with Qechua or the Spanish. The healing has to do with the frequency of the sound and the depth with which shamans are able to heal with that sound. They are facilitating the many unique facets of the ayahuasca root. Sound is significant in our world. There is a song in our heart, a Song of the Soul.

This Song of the Soul is a theory by which we can begin to understand what happens when an intrusive force—an intrusive energetic form—comes in and interrupts the music, the rhythm. The intrusive energetic form steals or blocks the frequency. It interrupts our ability to hear it. When a dark energetic form comes in, the ability to hear the Song of the Soul can be hijacked. That energetic form interferes in such a way that one may not be able to hear on an energetic level, the frequency of their Song of the Soul or rhythm, which is when and where problems start to happen. This is the energetic form given the name Mordrigal.

What happens next is we can become disoriented, disenfranchised from ourselves, disassociated, and depressed. We can lose our grip on our lives, and that's very specifically what we're talking about here in this book. Not in every situation, yet as an opportunistic, dark, energetic form, it can come in where there is a break in the fabric of the soul or the melody of the Song of the Soul. This energetic form then takes charge and begins playing its own dialogue, instead of the individual's own rhythm or melody. When one loses touch with their Song of the Soul, this could well be what depression looks like energetically. It interrupts the harmonies and the frequencies and then inserts an inner dialogue. That dialogue is intertwined with the identity of who you are as a spiritual being and as a human being. When this unwanted and unwelcome energy comes in and interrupts your ability to hear or connect to these harmonies and frequencies, that is phase one. In phase two, it starts to insert its own malevolent dialogue, which is where significant shifts and problems begin to present themselves. This is where Mordrigal takes hold and sets its claws into the unsuspecting individual.

The longer this type of interruption exists unattended, the deeper the set, the more challenging to defeat it, and the greater the difficulty to step past this intrusive energetic form. That is when, in its extreme form, it begins to tell individuals to do things that are not in alignment, such as to harm oneself or someone close to them. It is here where one begins experiencing negative thoughts about themselves, perhaps feeling intense shame that has resided within them, yet unrealized to that point in time. This dynamic is dealt with in-depth in the chapter entitled "Soul Fractures."

The Song of your Soul is the experience of only pure energy, light, and essence. It has no negative. The Song of the Soul would never say anything other than you are perfect and beautiful light energy. It is the truest, highest frequency of spiritual identity that one exists. An individual's Song of the Soul reminds them of their highest, purest spiritual essence. Thus, when this interruption occurs in its most intense form, it inserts a dialogue that overrides this higher frequency. The individuals are now getting this new word dialogue, in English or whatever language they speak, very specific to them individually. It is critical here to understand that the song does not stop. It is an individual's ability to hear it that is dramatically interrupted. It interrupts the frequency, but the song is still there.

There are degrees of interference from the Mordrigal

SONG OF THE SOUL

The CLIMAX: a 1919 movie featuring the music score 'Song of the Soul' energy. There may not be total interruption, not completely blocking the Song of the Soul all at once. Performing like a clogged artery, it is the degrees of involvement and how long Mordrigal has been allowed to exist. Some people have said to me, "I think I've had this all my life." Others have suggested a specific date when they felt they were hit, so to speak. DP's story suggests that a specific experience led to the sense of being hit at a specific moment or place.

At the beginning of this chapter, there is an opening rendition of "Song of the Soul," written in 1919 for the movie *The CLIMAX*, made in the same year. It was a very remarkable find, quite by accident. Years earlier, toward the ending time for a very large antique fair, I purchased a box of antique music scores, at the time when the vendor was tired and anxious to let go of any items before the task of packing up his goods. Recently, years later, I found the box and began searching for a very specific piece of music, to no avail. However, the next to last piece of music (a collection of roughly 75 music scores), lo and behold, this piece of sheet music presented itself. I was stunned, needless to say, in that I had been tossing around this concept of the Song of the Soul since I had begun writing. Then, there it was, the music score featuring the facsimile of the actors who starred in the film featuring the "Song of the Soul" composed 100 years ago! Too good to be just a coincidence. Synchronicity at its best.

CHAPTER 3

SHAMANS:
GATE KEEPERS
OF THE SOUL

Nisha pleaded with me, with her bright eyes looking up into mine, "I know what you're talking about. I experience this. Please, work with me?" This was following a two-hour lecture on the subject of this book.

Within two weeks or so, we began our work together. A few days before, a van hit a tree and the driver died on her front yard. She saw it all. Nisha was particularly burdened by an awareness of major events centering around death well before they were happening, including terrorist attacks. She had been isolating to a very severe degree, was sensitive to and internalized collective grief, had thoughts of suicide continually, and felt an eternal debilitating despair.

She was aware of very dark energies in her field as far back as 2010 when she suffered a severe head injury. Ongoing symptoms included a gigantic "energetic bump," as she called it, that hurt if someone stood a foot away. It actualized as severe pain in her left temple she described as feeling like a foot was pressing down on her head. In the years following her head injury, she kept banging her head as if "someone kept pushing me into things." Nisha mourned, never having experienced a successful, lasting relationship in the romantic domain. Most of her relationships were with men who carried "dark energy." Anything remotely promising turned sour within a very short time. Her vibrant, magnetic personality was overtaken by a feeling that something wanted her gone. Something was stopping her from feeling able to move forward with her life goals, expressing a feeling of a general pall over her life, believing she had pretty much always been miserable and never happy. During recent months, she experienced states of confusion and what she described as brain clutter.

Nisha was seeking relief and sovereignty over her destiny.

We agreed to a format of four to six sessions in as tight of a progression as possible. During the course of treatment, numerous insights revealed new layers to early childhood traumas, including a severe injury when she burned her feet as a result of being left in a bathtub at seventeen months old. Also, she experienced early sexual penetration by a family member around the age of five. Her story reflects one type of client who might be inclined to seek shamanic healing. Several soul retrievals and past life regressions were performed, and extractions were needed in each session. During much of our work, Nisha was too depressed to engage in life, yet she was deeply engaged in our process, taking the actions required for her to integrate our sessions. Her healing was profound and rapid. In a few short months, she dove into life with rigor and felt completely relieved of the energetic form referred to here as Mordrigal. She said that entity was "trying to take me out."

Nisha relayed her relief throughout the process that someone could actually understand her, see her, and know what was really going on. She felt a lifeline, and from our work together, she sensed the protections. The container aided her in doing the work on her end.

Nisha's situation called out for help, and it was necessary to respond to this call. In certain ways, it was Spirit asking me to show up at that moment. The complexity of Nisha's situation was rather profound, in that she was extremely well educated, highly dedicated throughout her history, and very committed to her family. Yet, she was living in absolute misery when I first met and began working with her. In so many ways, Nisha's story is that of the individual who has tried so many avenues of healing, yet has received very little relief, if any. This represents a rather typical type of condition that exists when an individual makes contact with a shaman, asking for assistance and help. It is the moment of realization that something greater is going on than what is observable to the naked eye. In her case, she was suffering at the first layer with the dark energetic form described herein as Mordrigal. Her treatment was, again, intense and rapid. She worked intensively during and between sessions, knowing and understanding that the work was hers—and as she states, it was for me to provide the container.

Shamanism is working in the unseen world, the unknowable world, the unspeakable world. Shamans are able to see, know, and speak when others are unable regarding realms that are not readily observable. Traditionally, shamans work when individuals reach out for assistance. A shaman is a healer in the deepest, truest sense of the word. In the history of shamanism, Michael Harner devoted much of his life to researching shamanism throughout the world. The shaman would receive a bag of potatoes or two chickens for the session work they did. The shaman did the work after returning home from their daily work. They were called on to fix things when there was a drought, or fix things when people were unsafe, or the community became unsafe due to some exterior attack that no one could really identify. A shaman goes to work when they are asked to work, and only when asked. Shamanic teaching predates religion. Shamanism is a practice and not a religion. Shamans, throughout history, have often been called to be warriors. Now may be a time in history when shamans, once again, are called to be warriors for the era we are in today.

As mentioned in the introduction, there was a kind of warning, or alert, given that there is very little attention paid to the dark side of energetic work. Dark energies exist in the energetic world just as they exist in the real world. I am always concerned to see or hear mostly thoughts around love and light, viewing the shamanic work as dealing on the light and fluffy side of things. There exist some very real dangers where caution and guard should and, actually, must prevail. There is a need for discernment when approaching the energetic arena, just as there needs to be discernment walking in daily life.

Now to journey through the world of shamanism:

WORKING IN THE GESTALT

Gestalt is defined by Webster's Collegiate Dictionary (1990) as *a structure, configuration or pattern of physical, biological or psychological phenomena so integrated as to constitute a functional unit with properties not derivable by the summation of its parts.*

When an opportunity presents itself to work with the extended environment, any time, it is always one of the richest types of intervention strategies and can be most enjoyable and effective. It is looking at the relationships within the family structure, when such information is available, from a whole perspective as one of the first ingredients of any story. The second ingredient is to determine the attitude with which individuals enter into session work. That is to say, when individuals participate with a strong intention of healing, that is exactly what tends to happen. The inverse is also operational if they do not believe in the work.

THE ROLE OF INTENTION

The important role of intention cannot be overstated. The intention of healing, of doing the work necessary to heal, is most positive in a shamanic context or otherwise. The client who, in some way, wants to be fixed is not a good match in that shamans engage in holding sacred space so that their client can safely do the work needed to heal. The only person who can heal is the person themself. The shaman facilitates the healing with strategies and seeing to one degree or another, while the client brings to the session what the work is that needs to be addressed.

In all likelihood, practitioners would agree that the intention to heal plays a major role always in the successful outcomes of therapeutic interventions, no matter the context or professional orientation. Fixing a person is not something that can be done, no matter the desire or intention of the healing professional. It is the individual who must come forward with the desire and intention of becoming well and realizing that the work, at the end of the day, is always theirs. One of the first shamans I ever worked with said, almost coyly, "Well, you know people who have done some work in their life…" meaning, I suppose, working in the psychological domain, the symbolic domain, "…they tend to benefit more from this work." I think what she was saying to me was if you are the one who showed up and said, "I'm ready to do my work, and I'd like you to assist me with this," you are going to get a lot done.

LEVELS OF UNDERSTANDING
(THE SHAMANS' PURVIEW)

One way to describe shamanic healing is by thinking of our perceptions in the world through levels of understanding. The levels become a way of viewing and understanding the world when we are more or less in the diagnostic phase of looking at a situation or evaluating what a person's needs are. The first level is where our most basic needs are met, one aspect being the very real situation where one needs to go to a physician. The analogy of a broken bone works well when considering this first level of understanding. One goes to a physician to receive the necessary remedy. I had good fortune some fifty years ago to have an orthopedist who was able to put steel rods in the center of the bones in my left forearm, and it worked. I was so glad I had access to the natural medicine of the bone doctor, where most of the Western medicine works best.

The second level of understanding is thought of as symbolic. That is the world of—going back to the analogy of the arm— "Why did my arm get broken? Why me? What caused this?" And so, one might go to a therapist to talk about those traumas that we mentioned earlier in this work. What happened, and why did that trauma happen to me? This aspect of understanding has existed particularly since the time of Sigmund Freud and Carl Jung as the founding fathers of insight-oriented therapies and the interpretation of human behavior. This is the domain of the symbolic approach to understanding.

The third level is referred to as where the "soul" resides. If one were to reach out at an arm's length around their entire body—above them, below them—that is essentially the

definition of their luminous energy field. It might go to
infinity. However, for everyday use and consideration, it is
within an arm's reach, almost physically palpable. We all
have a luminous body. When people talk of auras or energy
being around us, that is what is being spoken of. Back to the
broken bone analogy. When the bone was broken, with issues
regarding why the event happened, and why it was me that
fell into this circumstance, I was also wounded in this soul's
level of existence. That energy level, that energy bubble, was
also broken and hurt; the memory was stored at this level as
well. After years and years of interventions and talking about
the event and telling my story a hundred times, and being sick
to death of the story, it was when I stepped into the shamanic
understanding of healing that I finally was able to mend and
heal, and then give up the story. It was ever so necessary to
heal at the soul's energy level as well. That is when the deep
healing happened, about some forty years after the initial
event. I have noticed over these years that there are wounds
that have seemed impervious to healing. It is here where
shamanic interventions go beyond the traditions evident in
the Western medicine paradigm.

The fourth level of understanding is the level of pure energy.
The easiest way to describe this level is to describe it as the
energy of pure light and love. It's the energy of Spirit, Great
Spirit. There is a purity that exists at this fourth level. What
does the healed state look like for the client? This level of
understanding is reflected by perceiving the best of intentions
to forgive, to love, to be present every minute of every day.

These levels of understanding are accessible to one degree or
another for every individual. The shamanic practitioner learns

to look at the different levels simultaneously and then determine diagnostically where the most considerable emphasis needs to be directed within their client. Once these understandings are internalized, it becomes an automatic process of observation. For the shamanic practitioner, the primary work resides at the soul's level, as that is the realm where seeing into the unseen world requires that knowingness of the seer.

CHAKRAS

Every one of us has a chakra system that connects our physical body to our luminous energetic field. Chakras and chakra systems are universal, with only perhaps one or two exceptions within any of the major traditions, including most religions. About an arm's length distance surrounding the entire physical body is the approximate way to envision the energetic field or bubble that every single individual carries with them. Every minute of every day, every breath, the energetic field is present. It is where the bulk of work for the shaman takes place. The luminous body is where the Song of the Soul resides. The chakra system is the vehicle for understanding the overall health of the connection between the physical body and the higher self, the luminous energetic body.

Chakras are energy centers within the body. There are seven main chakra centers on the body. Secondary chakras primarily exist at the many connective joints within the structure of the body. The first chakra is generally referred to as the root chakra, meaning that it is at the lowest extremity of the torso, within the genitalia area of the body. The first chakra is associated with earth, the color red, and has a great deal to do with an individual's survival and procreation. The second chakra is located about two fingers below the navel or belly button, associated with the element of water, the color orange, and sexuality. The third chakra is at the solar plexus, or stomach,

THE CHAKRA SYSTEM

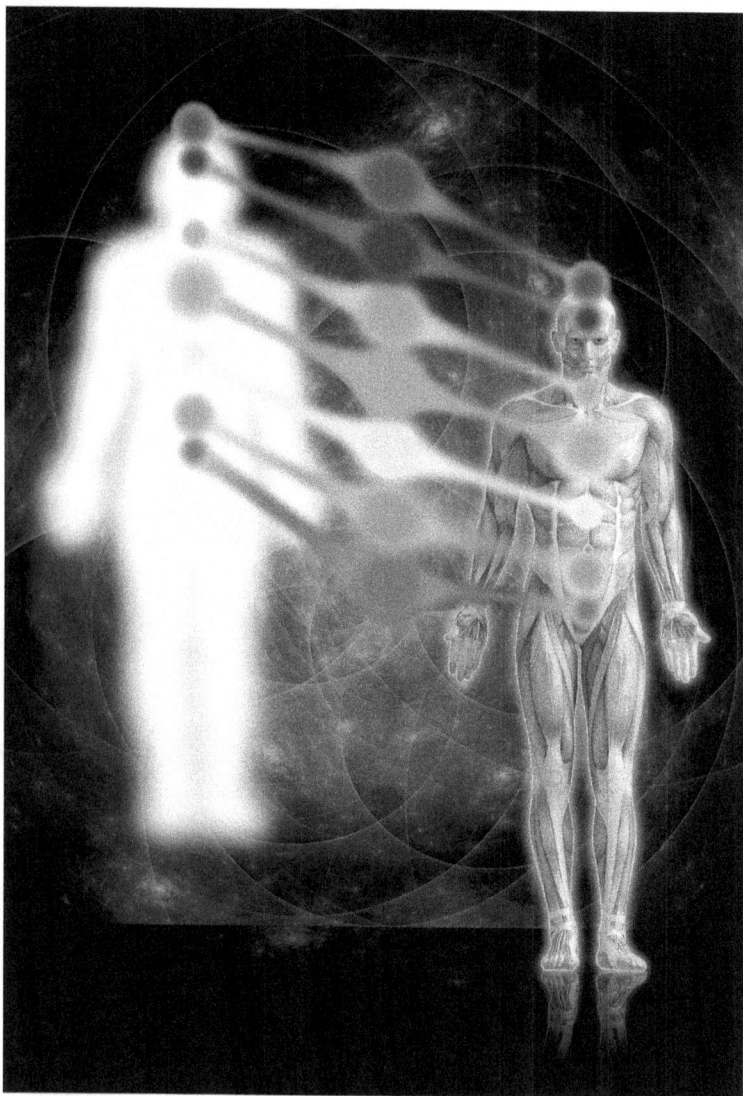

Connection of the Physical Body to the Luminous Body (The Soul's Eminence)

associated with the element of fire, the color of yellow, and the holding of power. The fourth chakra is at the heart, associated with air, the color green, and of course, love. The fifth chakra is at the throat, associated with light, the color blue, and with our ability to express ourselves. The sixth chakra is located at what is called the third eye or forehead, associated with pure light, indigo in color, and the act of seeing. Finally, the seventh chakra is at the crown, or the top of the head. It associates with knowingness, the color violet, and ethics at the grandest level.

One way to approach the understanding of how chakras function is to read them with a pendulum, paired with an object holding the client's energy, being held over each chakra. The chakra then reflects through the movement of the pendulum its health or operation, particularly concerning why a client may have come to see the shaman. An example might be severe anxiety or fear around a specific issue or topic that has been prominent for the individual over a period of time.

When the shaman holds the pendulum over the chakra, there are typically three possible conditions that may be reflected. Anywhere from four to ten inches away from the surface of the body, as the pendulum is held over each of the seven chakra locations, the pendulum will go into action, including no action at all. Should the chakra be healthy and fully operational, the pendulum will be swirling in a clockwise direction. The second possibility, the pendulum over a given chakra might not move at all. That would reflect that the chakra is compromised to the point where it is shut down and nonfunctional. The third condition, with the pendulum held over the chakra, could be going in a counterclockwise direction, meaning that the chakra is working in reverse order and therefore is operating in great fashion. I often liken this third condition of a chakra moving counterclockwise as being similar to a radar dish that is receiving any signals available to the frequency that the client has been dealing with, saying symbolically, "Come on in!" The first situation of the pendulum circling in a clockwise direction is the desired indicator that all is well with that chakra, particularly in relation to the issues presented. Both of the other two conditions of the closed chakra and the wide open chakra going in reverse direction give a strong indication that this is where and in what manner the client is holding the energy of the issue at hand.

That is the first-level assessment in knowing what the shaman and the client are going to be dealing with. It is at the end of any healing session that the final look is for each chakra to be, in my words, swinging wildly and robustly in a clockwise direction. I often describe this final action of the pendulum as looking like that of a helicopter blade ready for takeoff. The energies have been cleared, and the connections between the physical and energetic bodies have become robust. In later sections herein, it will be very understandable why that final action is something to cheer.

HEALING SESSIONS

In a typical healing session for the energy of the issue that is most prominent, one or more of the chakras will reflect where and how the energy is being held. If the pendulum is going in a clockwise rotation, then I would eliminate that chakra as holding any of that energy. If a chakra is closed or going in a counterclockwise direction, then I would consider those chakras as holding the energy that the client came in to deal with, usually negative in nature. Much energetic release can be realized by removing energy from the identified chakra or chakras. In Qechua, it is called hoocha, and when removing the stagnate energies, giving it to the Pachamama or Mother Earth is where that energy can be re-distributed to where it can be utilized more productively. It may seem a bit abstract, however, it is a primary strategy as a healing modality for this work. It is a matter of releasing the energy from the client's field that no longer serves their highest good.

The type of interaction described above is the beginning, and often the ending point for a healing session. It is between these two points where many additional journeying and extraction techniques are applied by the skilled and trained shaman.

CHI & LIGHT

We can always return to our purest essence, no matter how far it may feel from us. That is hope. It is often the piece that is missing from many of the teachings in the energetic healing field. It is challenging to find a positive way to place this information in a palatable, digestible manner. Reflections on darkness, despair, dead ends, the points of no return, particularly when addressing those issues as reflective of the dark side of energy, just simply are difficult at best. Of course, there is always hope, always light. Light is the energy, the chi. It is the life force energy of the planet.

There may be an agenda for darkness. If there is more darkness, then it may be increasingly possible to think there is a need to find more protection. On the literal level, that could involve purchasing weapons of one kind or another, security systems, and the like to increase the feelings of security. Perhaps it stimulates a desire for greater levels of healing. Darkness generates money, sales, economies, wars. If people believe that darkness is taking over, that it is somehow triumphing over light, they will act differently than when they realize that is fundamentally an impossibility. The power of light—the power inherently based in a healthy connection to one's luminous energy field, their Song of the Soul—is absolutely enormous.

TRUTH

For well over 2,000 years now, there has been an illusion that darkness may be prevailing. Darkness uses propaganda to say that it's winning, but it is not. I would say it is essential to remember to remind people of the truth. The truth is that light energy is infinitely more powerful than dark energy. There are elements of light energy that are much smaller percentage-wise than the dark elements that can completely explode a dark atom. It's proven in the world of physics. Light is far more powerful in even the smallest concentration than dark matter. But darkness can be much louder. It is fearful with its louder voice. It has a higher volume. It turns up the volume. It has the words and dialogue that can mimic our inner voice. Therefore, darkness is more effective at propaganda, but it doesn't mean it is necessarily triumphing over light. It is just louder. I feel it is important to remind people of that because, then, hope comes in. If you just acknowledge and empower, whatever is light that is within you, you will have the strength and the protection to prevail. We choose what we listen to. We are in a time (maybe we always have been) where there is a great deal of dark news, news that is not healthy. I sometimes turn it off and turn to music.

There are certain truths resting in ancient wisdom. That truth is that light is constant and unwavering, that light from the stars travels millions of years before we ever see it. If it could be interrupted, we would never see it. It travels through time and space for us to perceive. That is light's frequency; its ability to be perceived is unwavering. Unwavering time and space, the natural world, there is this empowerment that comes from remembering the truth.

TIME DIMENSIONS

The shaman dances on the equal sign (=) between the two worlds of the ordinary reality and the purely energetic realm of seeing. The ordinary reality world deals with linear time, which is living by a schedule that allows us to keep appointments, know when to go to bed and when to awake, and so on. Linear time keeps us on track.

The energetic realm requires that the shaman enter into the world of circular time where linear time has no place. In the circular time zone, travel is allowed in another dimension. Here, the shaman may journey back in time, often referred to as going into the underworld. By this statement of going into the underworld, I usually clarify this as traveling back in time, specifically to the places where soul wounding may have taken place. It is here that the saying "paying for the sins of our fathers when we have no idea of what those sins were" directly applies. This is the beginning definition of one of the most fundamental aspects of shamanism, that of shamanic journeying. It is here, within this concept of timelessness, that much healing takes place within the shamanic realm.

In a like manner, the gifted shaman may also travel forward in time, to the place of destiny. The statement here would refer to going into the upper world, which, like going into the underworld, depicts the ability to journey into the future, to the other side. There is a general tendency to be quite guarded in speaking to this aspect of shamanic journeying, particularly in that this portends a possible intrusion into sacred aspects of most organized religions. Here, again, it might be thoughtful to remind the reader that shamanism is a practice as opposed to being a religion in any respect. The type of work described here, this type of journeying, requires a shamanic practitioner that is highly trained and the holder of rather advanced skills.

REMEMBERING SOUL PARTS (SOUL RETRIEVAL)

Now, continuing with the concept of shamanic journeying, "re-membering" aspects of the soul, the parts that may have broken away during a wounding crisis, can be reconnected. It is like a part of the soul knew that a particularly egregious act was taking place, and the healthy part of the soul separated off. This soul part was then waiting for a time when it could be re-united with the original soul in a healthy manner. It is a universal type of knowledge of knowingness, unconsciously, that what was happening at a specific time was incorrect. Here, a kind of knowledge exists in another realm, one that we are not aware of at the time of the wounding.

We are not just re-membering; we are remembering the truth. If an individual has shattered (fallen apart), it is possible to re-assemble those parts. In the shamanic world, it is possible to be reconstituted. There is an understanding, an underlying belief in the shamanic field that what is broken down, dead, or destroyed can be reassembled, reconstituted, removed if necessary. The soul can go back, revitalized, rebirthed to an energetic original essence. If that belief weren't true, then shamans wouldn't or couldn't do much healing.

One of the more prominent pieces I have read or known in shamanic literature is a process referred to as a shamanic dis-memberment, particularly as part of an initiation. The soul longs to reconnect to any piece of itself. It does not want any particle outside of its container. I am talking here about re-membering, about bringing parts of the fractured soul back together. We can do that in the shamanic world, by honoring that there is a phenomenon called soul retrieval, which I also think of as remembering, or re-membering, the parts of the soul that have fractured off.

Soul parts from other lifetimes can also be re-membered or retrieved. Pieces of the soul have a similar unique frequency to that of the Song of the Soul. In essence, there is a homing device that they recognize. These separate "soul" pieces know each other, of course. The soul must have a homing device that also connects one to their past lives and then to their future as well.

ASSEMBLAGE

From a discussion with one of my clients, I was asked, "Did you say a homing device?" And my response was, "Yes. What happened was, there was a homing device that pulled the parts back together when we wanted to re-member. That device seemed to have pulled it right back into where it belonged. It needed and wanted to be reconstituted, the 'soul' part needed to be re-remembered. There is a natural order for the way things go; things always naturally drive to restore themselves to that order.

"Perhaps there is a connection to the natural way of how turtles swim a thousand miles to return and lay eggs where they were born. How do they know how to get back? How do migratory birds know where to go? They don't understand migration. It does not seem that scientists know what it is that pulls those animals back to their beginnings, but they go back to their beginnings, their original land. Maybe there's a connection here to speak to the natural world, to migration. We are migrating back to our beginnings, to our creation. We return then to ourselves, to our song that is there waiting for us."

This is the knowledge about the shamanic way.

SYNCHRONICITY

There is a strong belief held by many that nothing happens by accident, that everything is masterfully organized and happens with purpose. Being here at this moment in time isn't an accident; it was all part of the synchronicity of bringing this information forth. There is little room in this way of thinking that there is such a thing as a freak accident. Things happen for a reason. They happen by a greater scheme than what we typically give credit for. There is a plan—a master game—and it is present. That is where synchronicity comes into play; nothing happens by accident. Generally speaking, this is likely a primary tenet of the shamanic world as well.

As a shamanic practitioner and teacher, I believe a true shaman is one who when they are in a situation and they have to let go of every single preconceived notion they have of what's wrong, what's the matter, what's the treatment, they can turn it over to Spirit and say, "What do I do now?" A true shaman will call on Spirit, and Spirit will show up. Very interestingly, there is a contract that is made with Spirit. When Spirit is called on, Spirit will show up. The other side of that contract is when Spirit calls on the shaman, then they have to show up, just in the same way that Spirit shows up for the shaman. Many times, I have had myself booked very tightly with little unscheduled time available, and I receive an urgent request, which feels like an emergency. I treat it as Spirit giving me a call saying, "We need you, show up." I drop what I am doing, and I show up. That is the nature of this contract. In a like manner, right now, as you are reading this book, there is a contract in a certain sense that you are making. That contract with Spirit is that nothing in this book is going to be more than you can handle because it's just how it is. It's not going to be more than what you are ready for. If you have this book in your hands and you're reading it, it's time for you to read it, it's time for you to have this information. That's the nature of the contract that happens with Spirit, and that is the nature of synchronicity.

INTUITION

It is also a very abstract question to try to answer what role intuition plays in this work because it goes into the unseeing, unknown, and unspeakable realm—the realm that is walked as a shaman. Again, in the process, going back to the four levels of understanding, this manner of seeing becomes deeply embedded within the shaman's purview, so much so that every minute of every day, you are automatically working at those levels. It is a constant intuitiveness that is happening whenever a shaman goes into a session with a client. I often say, the real essence of the shamanic practitioner—and this is where experience comes in, and it does matter—is that in the energetic realm, Spirit will guide the practitioner in precisely what needs to happen. It is when the shaman can turn over all preconceived notions about their client and allow Spirit to guide their work. Then with the tools of the trained practitioner, the shaman is selecting the best and most appropriate, efficient tools to put into action, to go to work, and to know what needs to happen.

ARCHETYPES

There is a great deal of healing power in symbols and metaphors. When a shaman can see symbols, understand or apply a metaphor for something, then it becomes easier to shift and manage the energy through those representations. One aspect of the brilliant work I attribute to Alberto Villoldo is his translation, where archetypes are attached to abstract concepts. He is the master of connecting the thought of one's chakra to an archetype that then causes that chakra to take on a more palpable feeling aspect, which one can then more readily put their arms around. For instance, the idea that a jaguar archetype is in your second chakra and that archetype of the jaguar protects you and tracks for you creates an entirely different perception. Suddenly, the idea of your second chakra has a new and tangible scent or palpable feeling.

Additionally, when journeying in circular time, when traveling back in time to the past, there is a structure that provides guidance that keeps one from getting lost. It also allows for the systematic healing of past traumas in a very pragmatic manner. This is part of a concept where shamans follow maps and create new ones when needed. When journeying in the underworld or upper world, it is critical not to get lost; thus, the map concept is viable and most important (Alberto Villoldo, *Shaman, Healer, Sage* [New York: Harmony Books, 2000]).

MYSTERY SCHOOLS

Not all shamanic journeying is as structured as that brought forth by the Four Winds training. The late major historian and archeological researcher in the field of shamanism is Michael Harner. I encourage, if you are interested, further research by reading one of his works. He writes about the contrast between ordinary reality and non-ordinary reality. His journeying and techniques are quite unstructured, yet highly valid for that particular mystery school category. By using that term, I'm referring to these categories of tradition. When they're mystical in nature, when they deal in the unseen realms, they typically fall into the broad category of mystery schools. The tradition that I study comes from the ancient Incan lineage. It may go back thousands of years. I don't think we know, quite frankly. There has been increasingly validated speculation that the Sun Empire was more significant than the Roman Empire, covering most or all of South America. Different people have brought forth concepts, traditions, and lineages within the shamanic realm.

Alberto Villoldo founded the Four Winds Society and became one of the main people responsible for the translation of the ancient Incan tradition to the Western world. He brought together many aspects of modern thinking and practice that could be applied to our current times in the Western world. Dr. Villoldo has been the primary teacher for my development in this field. He is not only a profoundly apt shaman, he also writes extensively about shamanism and has authored so many books in the field that I have lost count.

Others, such as Sandra Ingerman, the Huicho tradition from Northern Mexico, and the writing of Carlos Constaneda, are reflective of other traditions. The many traditions written and taught fall into the broad category of being mystery schools. From my position, I hesitate to make a judgment that one is better than another. I just chose to study and practice in the Incan tradition, as translated to the Western world through the teachings associated with the Four Winds Society.

EXTRACTING AND INTEGRATING

When I work with a client, I am generally in the healing mode, taking things out that have been blocking people from self-realization. That is fundamentally the practice. That is the name of the game. It is not that I am going to give you something that I think you need, an energy, from out in this esoteric realm. As a rule, shamans extract and integrate, but do not add. I cannot think of exceptions to this. When a client offers that someone put such and such into their field, then I know that I will be in the mode of operation where I'm undoing another person's work. That has happened in my experience.

Three types of energetic extractions routinely take place when working with a client. These are fluid, crystallized, and underworld. It is generally not appropriate to go deeply into what these are, other than to give brief descriptions here. A fluid energetic form could be considered as something attached that was more or less floating by, or even placed directly upon one without their awareness. It might be something random, could be an intrusive energetic form, or even perhaps some aspect of a friend or relative that had an issue they were struggling with regarding a relationship with them. The second form is that of the crystallized energy, where once wounded directly in a previous lifetime, that wound might tend to repeat, from lifetime to lifetime, as some of us might be able to consider. Within this category, we may find cords, which are quite interesting in and of themselves. Cords can be linkages to anything from someone deceased, a past relationship, a family member, a strong belief system. The third type of extraction rests in the underworld and the domain of the trained shaman. Briefly, it deals with the areas where wounds have taken place and the removal of aspects of those wounds. Admittedly, this is quite brief and is included here as a partial description, not intended to provide an in-depth explanation. This is the type of information and skill development that is attained through in-depth training in the shamanic field, no matter the mystery school attended.

Thus, an essential concept that the shaman must deal with is what is on the surface before dealing with what exists in the other deeper esoteric realms, those issues found through journeying. The most magnificent interventions in the underworld will have little purchase if the energetic forms, cords, or any other issues residing on the surface of the client are not dealt with first. All other interventions will not be useful when there are surface issues left unresolved. This most critical concept I suspect generally applies throughout most of the helping professions. The opening vignette in chapter 5 refers somewhat to this concept and is again visited more in-depth within chapter 7.

FIND A SHAMAN

How can you tell that the shaman you're working with is having a positive impact on your life? The answer to that is pretty direct. Trust your instincts and ask yourself the question, "How do I feel?" How do you feel when you have completed a session with this person who you have chosen to be your shamanic practitioner? If the answer is you feel lighter, refreshed, uplifted, hopeful, calm, peaceful, positive, then those are pretty strong indications that the person you are working with is having a significantly positive influence on your life.

Conversely, if you walk out of a session feeling tense, anxious, crying, or in pain, chances are that the person you are working with may be operating outside of any lineage and training and that, in fact, you may have been subjected to a session that is less than helpful, or perhaps the practitioner is inexperienced. Above all, you have to trust yourself. Further, it is not always the right time or the right combination of practitioner and client.

There are some very clearly recognized, well-documented lineages that exist to train Westerners to become shamanic practitioners. As a consumer, you might want to research how long the individual you are considering has been working in the shamanic field. How many clients has the practitioner worked with? What has their experience been? What types of energies has he or she worked with? What have they seen in their clients?

They don't need to give you any names, but you could easily ask them questions about what their experience has been following their training, and what the base of their training was.

I had a very profound learning, probably one of the most significant learning experiences on the trail, to becoming a competent shamanic practitioner. It was with a client who left the healing session crying. It was early on in my learning, like all shamans in training where they are asking all of their family and friends to allow them to work on them to begin the learning process. In this case, her leg had been severed in a past life. I'm working with her, and all of a sudden, there's no connection between the leg and her body, and I just did not know what to do. I was lost. She left the session crying.

Following a discussion with my mentor, I called this client three more times to see if I could make the needed repair that had left her crying. It was direct and straightforward. Her leg needed to be reconnected energetically. The third time I called, I said, "This is the last time I'm calling you. Please come back to see me." She did. I reconnected her leg to her body, and when she got up, ready to leave, she said, "You know, that leg has never felt right. I never felt like I had my legs under me." It was a learning process, so it doesn't necessarily mean that I did something terrible. I was in a learning stage. It can be inexperience and not knowing what to do as a practitioner. That is what I mean when I say experience does matter in this work. It does.

REMOTE INTERVENTION

It is always interesting to note that when dealing in a strictly energetic world, remote work is as effective as direct in-person intervention. In the client story shared in the next chapter, the clients live on another continent. How could I be intervening with them on a different continent? Much to the collective pleasure of all involved in this work—client and practitioner— the energetic field is readily available regardless of time or distance. I would estimate that no less than 90 percent of my caseload is remote, covering locations throughout the world. It is the ability to deal remotely that allows for this. It is a gift, among other things, that our technological world brings to us: internet applications that allow for no-cost international connections. Totally remarkable.

The remote intervention takes place by asking the client to blow into a stone the energy of what it is they wish to deal with, and then at that very moment, their luminous field enters the working space. At that point, I utilize the pendulum in the same manner described above in the "healing session" description. I find it necessary to be connected through the telephone for the duration of the remote session. I am aware that some practitioners feel they can work remotely without the benefit of the direct connection. This points to the universal reality that there is more than one way to accomplish the same outcomes, again depending on the training and the tradition.

A SHAMANIC WARRIOR

Think of the story of Indiana Jones. As an archeologist in his pursuit of the goal, Jones encounters every imaginable barrier one could think of. Indiana Jones is on a quest and determined to prevail, no matter what the cost. It is an archetypal story. Like Indiana Jones in *Raiders of the Lost Ark*, shamanic practitioners go on a quest to facilitate the healing process, being in service and working to access the highest self in their clients. Similarly, the shaman does not quit until the work is done, which can mean within a specific session or on through to the most profound healing that takes place over time.

The teaching involving the content within this book around the Mordrigal energetic form has only been taught at the advanced shamanic skill level. That is not to say that much of this knowledge should not be taught earlier in the process of learning shamanic skills. It reinforces the notion that this subject area resides on the dark side of energetic teaching and therefore has had a tough time seeing the light of day, as far as mainstream teaching goes. It is ever so much more pleasant to stay with the rainbow and butterfly's avenue of perceiving and learning.

The shamanic warrior is the practitioner who has developed a maturity, having little to do with age. The saying that a 13-year-old can be very mature and an 80-year-old incredibly immature applies here. It is the conscious ability to engage with compassion, sympathy with non-engagement, expanding through experience, knowledge of trauma often through firsthand experience. It is of extraordinary importance that the practitioner is experienced. The shamanic field requires one to be hands-on. Theory has little purchase without experience. Referring back to the concept where these teachings have only been given to the advanced student is for a good reason. It is a sophisticated level of intervention for the practitioner.

As noted in the quest of Indiana Jones not stopping until he found the treasure, the shamanic warrior does not stop until the situation is resolved. A most important caveat for the shamanic practitioner is that when something is observed or noticed, it is then activated. That means very directly that if a shaman sees it, the shaman has to then deal with it. Regarding teaching, a significant soapbox for me is if something really should not be there, then remove it, get it out. The shaman carries the tools, so use them.

Regarding energetic forms of all makes and descriptions, the fact that we are in our bodies, have presence through our physical being, including the same for our clients, we always have the upper hand. The energetic form is attempting to get a free ride, as that energetic form does not have a physical ability or presence. This is a distinction that if one can internalize the concept, then the anxiety should ideally decrease. Both the client and the practitioner always have the advantage. By my observation, it is mostly fear that gets in the way. Thus, the shamanic warrior is fearless, knows the terrain like the back of their hand, and understands the serious nature of what is at hand.

The next chapter is entitled "Mordrigal" and delineates major facets of this energetic form. One might understand why the section entitled "Warrior" is included here, as it applies almost directly to the intervention and healing from this most devastating and unwelcome energetic form.

CHAPTER 4

MORDRIGAL

The broad considerations at this point delve into psycho/ spiritual dynamics. This mostly refers to the thought that often, one of the first things I would say to a client is, "You're not crazy." The palpable relief that could be seen on their face would be overwhelming. I would say this to the client once I could see that the Mordrigal energetic form was on them. Just as recently as the day I am writing this, during a "potential client" phone consultation, the following description took place: "I can't move forward. I am having feelings of anxiety, panic, fear, terror, and depression. I get lightheaded and dizzy to the point that I had to take sick leave from my job. I am held back by this attack. I cannot move forward."

There are many symptoms prevalent when viewing the presence of the Mordrigal energetic form. These symptoms can include items such as sleep deprivation, night terrors, implants, auditory hallucinations, depression, and feelings of fighting for one's life. Here, the primary consideration is being invaded by an intrusive spirit energy, most often referred to as an entity. Throughout this book, I have carefully referred to an entity as an energetic form. My sense is that the word entity conjures up misgivings that are not productive to the overall treatment for the energetic invasion of an unwelcome, unwanted energetic form.

One client described Mordrigal, this energetic species, in the following manner: "The most basic aspect of this entity is to get the individual to distrust who they are." There are always physical manifestations. Another example is of a family where each member experienced the same pattern and similar physical manifestations. The father spoke throughout treatment as experiencing severe itching in the genitalia area of the body and his foot, being poked in both eyes, inflammation at the armpit during the day or night, experiencing pokes with red dots that would disappear an hour or so later.

The mom felt pokes in both eyes, the backs of both ears, and felt as though particles were being drilled into the eyes, giving her pulsing headaches. Pokes just below the collar bone and right breast hurt and were accompanied by a severe itch on both armpits.

Their daughter found her head constantly spinning, much phlegm and pain in the neck area, both ankles hurting, and complaints about both feet hurting. Initially, the grandmother was also involved in the treatment, her symptoms being translated by the mother because the grandmother only spoke Mandarin.

This is an example of treating a family viewed from the gestalt perspective. It was in the middle of 2011 when I was contacted with an assistance request that read as follows: "Hi Peter, R___ has a client that is under attack intensively can you help?"

This turned into a two-year tag-team intervention involving the husband and wife, their daughter (age eight at the time), and the grandmother (mother's mother). This family lives on another continent and is of Chinese descent. Their situation was one of intense discomfort on all levels. This was an intervention early on with discovering the essence of what came to be known as Mordrigal, yet so early in the identification that a formal protocol had not yet emerged. However, it is to point to this series of interventions as perhaps the most informative at this early stage of identifying what this most unwelcome and invasive energy was all about.

The most unusual identifier was that all four presented exactly the same pattern of functioning, or in their situation, non-functioning chakra systems. The typical pattern for understanding the chakra systems, as noted in chapter 3, was not present. It was also absolutely unheard of at that time that all chakras would behave in a precisely similar pattern, and to boot, each member of the family presenting the same pattern. The pattern presented by the pendulum was also very unusual. It was the first real perception that something highly dysfunctional was going on within this family structure, energetically speaking. The unusual pattern was that all seven chakras were going in the same direction and all seven changing direction the next time going over the chakras, through to the third pass over the chakras, all seven not moving at all. That pattern would repeat endlessly. Chapter 7 goes in-depth about the protocol that emerged over time from these early observations.

A primary characteristic for the family was that they never, so much as for one moment, considered that what they were experiencing to be centric to any kind of psychological disorder. This is important because, to that point in time, most clients presenting this pattern and degree of discomfort had an absolute tendency to internalize their situation, and either they or those close to them would declare some type of psychological disorder to be present. This phenomenon was not present with this family.

What emerged over time was that persistence mattered. They were dealing with a kind of overlay that disconnected each family member from their chakra system. The overlay concept will be delineated further as we go forth in the book. The outcome of the treatment was that once a very specific aspect of the extended family dynamic was revealed, their deep healing was experienced, and the intensity of the interventions declined to the point of their living in relative greater comfort. A great deal of formative learning took place at a very considerable cost to this family, for which the degree of gratitude and reverence for this family's commitment to wellness cannot be overstated.

It was during this period of intervention, stimulated by this very early exposure to the existence of some kind of energetic invasion, that opened the door to the evolution of this work. First and foremost, this energetic pattern interfered with the normal functioning of the chakra system. This then gave way to seeing the same pattern repeat itself, gradually increasing in frequency with other individual clients.

This resulted in the beginning awareness of the absolute need to reveal this phenomenon to a greater community. Since this period, where so much additional information became available regarding how to work with this energetic form, teaching around this phenomenon, and the realization of this book, it became an essential mission of mine to "out" this very devasting energetic form called Mordrigal.

One possible description of the overlay is that it functions in the same way a circuit breaker in your electrical control panel in your home does. When the overlay has victimized an individual, it breaks the connection between the physical body and the higher self or energetic body. The Song of the Soul gradually becomes unrecognizable, as it has been hijacked, interrupted. Just as the electrical circuit breaker cannot be turned back on until the short circuit issue has been resolved, so it is with this overlay that prevents one from functioning at their highest good or self. It is here that Mordrigal does its most devasting work with the most intense impact because one begins functioning without the benefit of the Song of the Soul. In the long term, this is one of the most damaging conditions an individual can experience in their life.

When I looked back through the data collected over the past fifteen years, there was a very clear turning point mid-year in 2013. Up to that point in time, I was aware of a very distinct pattern that was associated with the overlay concept, a series of implants, by my perception, that was also very systematic in their presentation, client after client. During most of any given session's work, the time was spent removing the overlay and then attempting to remove the perceived implants. It had been a folly to that point, in that as quickly as I might remove an implant, by the time I had moved to the next one, the previous implant would have already returned, almost as quickly as it was removed. Again, looking back at the data, as early as 2008, there is evidence of the presence of this energetic form, yet I had no idea of what was being observed. A typical session with this energetic form of Mordrigal being present was spent in the arduous effort to remove its implants while little time would remain available for the more profound healing work needed. By the time of working with the family described above, it became apparent that there had to be some kind of a control center located in the body. This projected control center would act like a "receiving or sending unit" that beaconed out a signal calling this Mordrigal energy back to the energetic field of the individual.

It was the turning point in 2013 while working with a

physician experiencing the Mordrigal energetic form that during his session, he turned to me and said the following: "My spirit guides want me to tell you to keep on doing what you are doing, however, you are looking in the wrong place." To this statement, of course, I responded, "Please tell me where I should be looking. (I was searching on the man's torso) He then led me to the base of the neck, which, when the energy was successfully removed at that location, then all of the other symptoms, specifically the pattern of implants, disappeared completely. As a result, this was the beginning emergence of a successful protocol of treatment for this most unwelcome, unwanted Mordrigal energetic form. First, to remove the overlay and second to locate and remove the sending or receiving unit control centers. The terms overlay and sending unit are woefully inadequate to describe their function of completely disabling the individual's ability to function in a wholistic manner. The point here may be that we truly need an expanded vocabulary to describe and walk in this most foreign territory. Please note that giving it a name does not make it a single entity. It is important to understand that this energetic form is a "species" of a very devastating energetic form.

How would one know if this dark energy is impacting their life? There are some clues that one might be able to follow to begin to understand if this could be a solution that perhaps an individual may have been seeking for months or even years. Often when I start to interview a client, I will ask the client if there are issues they are dealing with in their body. The responses cover a wide range of anecdotes ranging from having a particular pain and going to the doctor multiple times with no diagnosable cause, to having a piercing pain in one's ear or a throbbing pain in the big toe.

Perhaps there is some type of irrational thought plaguing an individual? One scenario may go like this: He or she may have been to see a psychologist, and the inquiry goes something like, "Did something happen to you? Did you have a trauma?" There may be something in the history. However, it is easier to say there is nothing that gives any rationalization for this intense fear or anxiety that has suddenly gripped the individual's life, at least that they are aware of. The therapist cannot find anything that explains it. Possibly it is taken up to the next level, and the psychiatrist may find it appropriate to prescribe medication.

Regarding the case of the Mordrigal energy being in play, instead of making the situation better, it makes it worse. Now one can find themselves sitting in their home and not sleeping at night because of constantly feeling like there is an intruder or invader ready to break into their home at any moment. They may look in the driveway, look at the street, and there is no one there. Yet, they still may feel this imminent energy is about to invade their home at any moment.

Calling the police for the second time this week will be to no avail because there is nothing there. There may even be a moment or two when, although an individual may not admit it to other people, they have sat in the parking lot of an emergency room facility because of knowing an emergency is imminent, yet it never happens. They want to save themselves a trip in the ambulance.

The very extreme version of this energy may require they check themselves into a mental health hospital. They may feel like they are going crazy, or in the darkest, most intense aspects of this, they have constant thoughts of ending their life— or worse, hurting someone near and dear to them. Perhaps they have even sought information from a suicide hotline. Again, almost impossible to trace what is triggering this, they know without any question that something is causing these thoughts. It is the inner dialogue that is going on within their psyche that is driving them to say things, isolate themselves, and feel fear, panic, anxiety, and even have suicidal thoughts. They know they must remove whatever it is from their lives.

The first thing is to reassure anyone reading this book that if they are getting full-body chills of confirmation, they may have identified a condition that has been happening and that they may have found an avenue to a potential solution as well. It is important to know that this energy can be removed from one's life, that it is possible to have a full recovery and move forward on the journey of their healing, whatever that may look like. Healing can happen.

This energy strikes when an individual is already low in their resistance. For example, if someone has experienced some type of abuse in their life, experienced family trauma, or any type of injury into their being, this then can manifest as the emotion of shame. This emotion of shame, in its essence, is an invitation for this energy to come into one's life. It is as if this energy scans individuals, finds the shame frequency, and says, "I have a new home, a new host. I have a new place that I can inhabit." Shame is one of the embedded invitations to this energy. Should one have shame from any of these types of events, then they may be sending out a sonar, a kind of unspoken and unintentional invitation to this energy to come into their life. Generally, what happens is no matter how bad an individual might be feeling from an actual event, this energy comes in and amplifies whatever that feeling is to make it feel 100 times worse. This is what is so insidious about this energetic form. The next chapter, "Soul Fractures," frames in-depth strategies for healing around specific kinds of events, specific phenomena around the emotion of shame.

The Mordrigal energetic form has the capacity to hijack one's inner dialogue, the song or knowing that one has within themselves, and replace that rhythm or hum with negative thoughts or words that suggest negative actions, fears, paranoia, anxiety, and possibly thoughts of suicide. The reason that this happens from an energetic standpoint is that this energetic form interrupts the ability to hear the Song of the Soul, which is one way of knowing one's true essence of who they are. Instead, Mordrigal replaces that song, rhythm, or hum with its lyrics that are designed exclusively to disrupt an individual's life and end it if possible.

If one could create a metaphor for the Mordrigal energetic form, it is like a bacterial infection that exists in the energetic world. It is a bacteria, so like all bacteria, this energy can be contagious to people who are susceptible to it. That means if one has a weakened immune system or a weakened protection system, then this bacterial infection in the energetic world can be picked up by an individual. In short order, the Sacred Shield plied against Mordrigal is equivalent to penicillin plied against a bacterial infection.

Like Ebola or a food-borne disease, the Mordrigal energetic form is an infection, or perhaps better said, an infiltration into your energy body. What that means, as with all things in the energetic world, is it's invisible in the mundane world. It is not readily detectable. It cannot be seen by the human eye nor picked up by conventional medicine. This is an affliction in the energetic world, the energetic field. The only solution to solve an affliction or a problem in the energetic world is to find someone who works within that realm. Just understanding that yes, it can be addressed, released, and one can go on with their healing journey is important. However, things that happen in the energetic world need to be addressed by people who work in the world of energy; in other words, a shaman— or better stated, a shamanic practitioner.

Shamans walk between worlds. They walk between the physical world and the energetic world; therefore, they can go into the unseen realms and work with an energy disease—an energy affliction. The shaman can adjust the frequency so that this afflicting energy can be extracted and removed, allowing one to go on, heal, and experience happiness and more light in their life.

To facilitate understanding of this energetic phenomenon and to place it in as understandable of a context as possible, the search for an appropriate name to represent this malignant energetic form began. Mordrigal comes from a combination of a musical term, a "madrigal," as a kind of "musical no man's land," that was first created by a morbid character named Gesualdo around 1600. He was known for murdering his wife most violently and perversely and getting away with it because of his royal designation. Along with additional perversions of extreme meanness throughout his life, and also as the creator and composer of the madrigal chaotic musical form, these two components come together in a very disharmonious way, not unlike the descriptions for this most unwelcome energetic form now referred to as Mordrigal. The "Mor" comes from morbid. It is about the frequencies that come together with the intent of creating destruction and death. That is where this name comes from.

The whole intent of this chapter is to define something that is essentially undefinable. Understand that this energy essentially goes into the library of an individual's subconscious, finds their fears, their experiences, anxieties, and then pulls those items that are most frightening and uses those issues to attack. Naming this energetic form as Mordrigal is an effort to attain a short reference to a very complex phenomenon.

Not knowing one's library, as a shamanic practitioner, it is impossible to know just how it will show up. However, to know that an individual is suffering from this Mordrigal energy can be accomplished by recognizing the pattern of the way the energy interacts with an individual on the external presentation, that of the chakra system or pattern reflecting the chakra connections to the higher self. How it manifests within the psycho/physical/spiritual domain is the puzzle the practitioner must begin to unravel. Much of the ultimate strategy then relates to the client's willingness to dig into their subconscious library of fear and shame.

The first step in any of this is recognizing that one may be susceptible to this type of energy. Traumas of one kind or another in one's life can cause a kind of "soul fracture." It is reckoning with the fact that one may have had trauma in their life. It could be framed as a soul fracture that has created an opening for the intense feeling of shame. Should an individual recognize that they may have a sensitivity or a portal through which this energy could or has entered, then their role, first and foremost, is to proceed with the full intention of healing.

Choose from this point forward to no longer be a victim of this energy. Choose to go on the journey of deep healing. That journey is going to heal an individual mentally, physically, emotionally, and spiritually. By working through the energetic field, the single biggest distinction that can be put forward is to choose to heal. Participation in the process, investing energy, resources, and a strong belief that it can happen, will be only beneficial. If an individual shows up with all of those ingredients, it will strongly suggest the extent possible that one can and will move on from this affliction, that it can be released. However, if an individual chooses to sit back and be cloaked, so to speak, with shame and fear, then this energetic attack could well continue to deepen and worsen until one finds themselves in a very, very dark place. Specific healing strategies are delineated in the last two chapters of this book.

Fear is most informative and delicious to this dark energetic form. Fear is what I refer to as a "banquet buffet dinner special" for this dark energy. It loves fear. Fear does not serve us, nor is it our friend. It is most important to learn to conquer it. Fear appears to be essentially irrational. Of course, there are situations where fear is appropriate. My observation regarding fear is that mostly it centers on the idea or belief that "If I do this specific thing, I might die." When one is asked to stop and consider what they are frightened of, by asking is the potential of dying likely, the answer will most often be that the outcome of dying is not likely to be the case.

Another thought that I have contemplated over the years is the statement that "you get what you fear." I first heard that statement some fifty years ago. What I think this means is that one puts so much effort into avoiding a certain outcome or situation that the energy then comes back as intention, which is then fulfilled due to the nature of placing so much energy into not having that certain thing happen, some kind of backfiring phenomenon. Focusing back on this dark Mordrigal energy, also considering other energetic forms of a similar nature, one might get a pretty strong notion of why fear is less than helpful. An individual, particularly those in a face-off with this most unwelcome, unwanted, malignant energetic form called Mordrigal, will do well to place a high level of management of their fear index. This discussion intends to create some understanding of the nature of fear. As shamanic practitioners, assistance can be provided by finding and reducing the intensity of some of the cases where the fear is based. This is not an easily managed aspect of treatment. But, it is probably the single most important domain in the overall strategy.

Three authors mentioned in the first chapter helped create a broader perspective around this Mordrigal energetic concept.

The first author is Simone Weil. That would be Weil in English, though she was French; thus, the French pronunciation is most appropriate, phonetically as "Vay." Simone Weil lived from 1909 to 1943, through two world wars and the Great Depression. She lived at an extremely pivotal time in history, a time of tremendous change and shifting in the global power structure.

One of my clients suggested that I look into her work. It was during those first moments when a separation took place for her beginning to realize the difference between herself and the energies of Mordrigal that she recommended Weil to me. This client described her situation very graphically as having been put in a chest, the chest is wrapped in chains, and then thrown to the bottom of the sea. When I first read some of the works written by Simone Weil at this client's suggestion, I was astonished by the high degree of similarity in her description of "the afflicted soul" and my clients' description of the Mordrigal energetic form.

Simone Weil used the term affliction to describe the presence of very dark energy. Weil defined affliction in many ways. Included here are some of the quotes from her collected works. Affliction is "a kind of human being who is neither alive nor dead. The afflicted individual is a compromise between a man and a corpse. He is of another human species" ("The Iliad, or The Poem of Force").

"*Affliction* is above all anonymous; it deprives its victims of their personality and turns them into things. It is indifferent, and it is the chill of this indifference, a metallic chill, which freezes all those it touches, down to the depth of their soul." Weil goes on to define how affliction gains its power: "They only fall into affliction if suffering or fear fills the soul to the point of making it forget the cause of the persecution." Here I would draw the reader back to the concept of a trauma, a trauma that may be blocked from consciousness over much of one's life, and further mention that if we consider the idea of past lifetimes, it may be that the individual does not even know of a trauma that has been carried forward. One further quote for consideration: "There is not real affliction unless the event which has gripped and uprooted a life attacks it, directly or indirectly, in all its parts, social, psychological, and physical. The social factor is essential. There is not affliction where there is not social degradation or the fear of it in some form or another" (George A. Panichas, ed., *The Simone Weil Reader* [Wakefield, RI and London: Moyer Bell, 1977], 440–445). It is most important to keep in your consideration, in that the most prevailing description common to all clients suffering some degree of the Mordrigal energetic form is that they are also suffering to varying degrees, isolation. More on this later.

The second author is Jack Forbes, born in 1934, and left this world in 2011. He was an American Indian thinker and founded the Native American Movement in 1961. He developed Native American studies programs across the country throughout his lifetime. He was professor emeritus and former chair of the Native Studies Department at the University of California at Davis. Forbes used the term wetiko to refer to a terrible energetic form long known to the Native Americans. *Wetiko* is a Cree term, referring to a cannibal, or more specifically, to an evil person or spirit who "terrorizes other creatures by means of terrible, evil acts, including cannibalism." Note: wetikos do not eat other humans, though in a symbolic sense they do. To get right to the point of his writing, perhaps to encourage one to explore his writings further, he argues that Columbus was a wetiko, that he was mentally ill or insane, the carrier of a contagious psychological disease, the wetiko psychosis. The native people were, on the other hand, sane people with a healthy state of mind.

We might reflect here on the wetiko energy as an energetic cannibal. Forbes goes onto say that Anglo-American imperialism is a form of cannibalism designed to eat Indians and also to consume the native people's land and resources. In his writings, he documents that the native Americans have been aware of this energetic form for many hundreds of years. Jack Forbes describes Hitler and Nazism as having consumed Jews, Poles, this wide swath of people, and attributes that to the wetiko energy and psychosis. He attributes essentially the last 2,000 years, more than 2,000 years, to the wetiko energy (Jack D. Forbes, *Columbus and Other Cannibals* [New York: Seven Stories Press, 2008], 22–25).

Abuse took place in Europe simultaneous to the Renaissance, ironically, when something referred to as witch-hunting occurred. This was a time of great suspicion that many women, in particular, were accused of being witches. It definitely met some of Forbes's criteria for cannibalistic-like behavior, literally taking people's lives in many cases. They were burning and drowning them if the suspicion was great enough. This is part of a history that we are hesitant to write about in our history books (Leonard Shalin, *The Alphabet Versus the Goddess* [New York: Penguin/Compass, 1998]).

Thinking that this dark energetic form, "wetiko, affliction, or Mordrigal," is just now manifesting is virtually not conceivable. This dark energy has been in existence for a very long time. We may be seeing it more readily currently with it being unveiled more and more. Writing about this dark energetic form now is about unveiling this energy in yet another manner, a manner in which we can more effectively deal with it. Jack Forbes did not, per se, know what to do with his wetiko energy other than to identify it. Simone Weil also did not know what to do with the dark energy of affliction yet described it in detail and did lean toward some manner of impacting it, the process of metaxu, which will come up later in this writing.

The third author here is Paul Levy. Paul Levy was born in 1956 and is very much alive today. He uses the term malignant egophrenia and uses wetiko and malignant egophrenia interchangeably. In his book, *Dispelling Wetiko*, he landed on wetiko as the one viable term to describe this extremely dark energetic form and relies on Jack Forbes's work as a groundwork for his thinking.

Paul Levy takes the name of wetiko and describes how wetiko—or malignant egophrenia—is ontologically real. It is non-local, which makes it nearly impossible to find this energy in its entirety, being nowhere and everywhere at the same time. Levy's work is extraordinary in that it furthers our potential understanding of this very dark form of energetic invasion that occurs within the individual's psyche. Levy describes the wetiko/malignant egophrenia as "existing outside of time, outside of place, a place that is not contained in a place, a placeless place located who-knows-where." He describes the place where this energy exists as being in a place that is not in the geography of our three-dimensional world. He declares that the question "Where?" loses its meaning altogether (Paul Levy, *Dispelling Wetiko* [Berkeley, CA: New World Library, 2013], 5). I fully agree with these descriptions of wetiko/malignant egophrenia as unbelievably accurate and similar to the energetic form I describe as Mordrigal.

The one thing all three of these authors have in common, who span more than 100 years in time in their writing, none of the three proposes how to deal with it. Paul Levy, to a certain extent, attributes some things to the wetiko energy that—and I'm taking much liberty here to do any interpretation of his work—this energy may be causing individuals, as well as societies and cultures, to have to deal with healing at a very deep level, to look deeply at who and what we are. That may be the case. However, there is somewhere between little and nothing that can excuse an energetic form that thrives on people killing themselves or takes advantage of people who have been in harm's way.

Within the 500+ energetic sessions dealing with this energetic form of Mordrigal (wetiko, affliction, malignant egophrenia), a protocol emerged as a means of working with this energetic form. What is proposed here, in this work, is a means to remove this energy from the individual. I like to say it is a simple protocol, although there is nothing simple about it. It requires a very mature practitioner, one who can and has confronted the fears in their life, a kind of "shamanic warrior." The ultimate goal of this book is to realize that there is a protocol to handle this and to promote a call for individuals to be cleared of these energetic states of being.

The condition apparent in the chakra evaluation that I see allows me to know if this energetic form is present. The representation is always the same. I never guess at it. I will hear people say I am not sleeping, and that is one indicator. However, the real key is when I hear people talk about being isolated. They have lost their friends, their family relations, they do not go out anymore, stay in their house, are afraid to go to the grocery store, and tend not to want any involvement with anyone. That is Mordrigal. That is wetiko. That is this dark energetic form.

Then most accurately, there is the pendulum that facilitates evaluating the operation of the chakra system. When the pattern presents itself, it cycles through and over all seven chakras going clockwise in the same direction. Then on the next pass over the chakras, all seven are going counterclockwise. This is then followed by all seven with no movement at all when going over the chakras a third time. This pattern then repeats seemingly on into infinity. When this happens, it is undeniable that the Mordrigal energy has taken over that client's essence, their being. If the energetic form is not there, that pattern does not present itself. At that point, then the client is clean and free from this particular form of energetic invasion. The treatment falls into the category of a more typical healing session found in the typical teaching strategies.

I have talked about how Mordrigal interrupts your ability to hear the Song of the Soul and how Mordrigal is so non-specific. It is nowhere but everywhere at the same time. I would say that this energy, because it is clever, has some aspect of ability for cloaking or invisibility. It attempts to hide when shamanic practitioners are trying to do work to expel it.

Shape-shifting might be one way to describe it, though it doesn't have any shape in the first place, yet it shifts all the time. As a practitioner, I have to pay attention constantly that it has not come back while in the middle of a client session. To summarize this, I am willing to put this out for people to see, read about, understand, and to hear, to the extent possible in this book, though holding the understanding that there are limitations to this format.

NOTE TO PRACTITIONERS: I'm saying if you're willing to read the first clues as a practitioner, if you're willing to look at patterns and say there's a specific pattern, if you're willing to trust that in 500 sessions there's a protocol that has emerged that works, if you're willing to accept that, then there is a whole pattern to follow that works to the benefit of your client who is suffering from this most alien force. I contend it is a simple pattern. It is quick. By that, what I mean is a practitioner can get this energetic form off the surface in relatively short order and then be afforded the ability to take the rest of the time available with your client to go in and do the deeper healing work with the soul fractures where this energy is likely rooted. Somewhat uncomfortably, I'm talking about going below the surface. This entity enters from the underworld, back in time, back through the family fracture, the soul fractures. It is necessary to work with this in the underworld. Every practitioner must have the skill and the ability to see it and deal with it also at that level. END NOTE.

There is an important concept of degrees of involvement, more or less of a pyramid, or I think of it as "degrees of succumbing to this energy." Three case examples come to mind. The individual who is treatable in one session, which is rare, though it does exist. Then there's a more recent series of successes. I call them successes because the clients have been able to attain in six sessions or less, getting this completely removed. These are important, in that from the perspective of having dealt with this energetic form of Mordrigal, over such a long and sustained period, this is more or less a significant breakthrough. In each case, the individuals were working at an intense level on their healing process and were deeply engaged.

And then going into an example of a more severe case, the client was completely fooled by Mordrigal, disguised as some great benevolent spirit that would bring enlightenment, then turning and being revealed as the nasty, devasting energetic form that it is. The claws were set so deeply that the course of treatment is long and very difficult. The process of separation of the soul from the energetic form is intense and requires consistent and deep work. In these more severe situations, the degree of isolation that the client experiences is profound.

Is it scaly, gelatinous, dark, shadowy? Is it cloudy? Is it reptilian?

I tend to avoid those terms in that they are not professionally oriented and can be frightening or unsettling. Suggesting, for instance, that a client has reptilian energy attached to them is pretty much something that I doubt any client wants to hear, yet that may be the exact description they offer of what they are suffering from. These are viable descriptions that I accept without reservation, yet I do not choose to portray this energetic form in that manner due to attempting to reduce overt anxiety around this issue.

In our history, humanity always tries to assign human characteristics to the unknown. We try to make God a man with long hair sitting on a throne in the sky. We try to make the energy of the earth a woman named Mother Nature. We try to assign human sensory characteristics to the unknown realm constantly. That is not something that can apply here. It is impossible to assign a human or earthly experience to this energy. One cannot call it scaly or demon-like because none of those descriptors apply.

Mordrigal is more of what I would call a pattern or an energetic structure that creates a blocking energy so that one cannot be connected to their higher self. It does not have any human characteristics that can be applied to it. It is more of a disrupting energy that has an intention to hurt an individual's self-identity. Of course, I think people want to know where this Mordrigal energy comes from, and the best answer after over 500 sessions is that it is most likely otherworldly. It presents itself, because of its vastness, more as a species of an energetic form, rather than just one entity. The name of Mordrigal, or wetiko, then represents a broad swath of energetic form as opposed to being just one energy. It comes from another source and utilizes a technology that we have no idea how to handle. By utilizing the name Mordrigal, it is an attempt to provide means to identify this ubiquitous energetic form that is indeed greater than just one energetic form. It is in reference to a species.

The descriptions go from A to Z, or they go from zero to 100,000, and everything is nothing. The minute you say it's reptilian, it's not reptilian. It will shift. What I would say about this is one has to remember that this energy has no designated form. The form that it adopts comes from one's consciousness or subconscious, where the experience of what is terrifying, repelling, or uncomfortable to the individual is defined and taken up by the Mordrigal energetic form.

Thus, if individuals hold inside of their awareness some frightening aspect, then Mordrigal takes on that identity and pushes to the extreme. Remember, this phenomenon of Mordrigal hijacks one's awareness, their consciousness. It goes into the subconscious as its private library and brings forth the fears, making them real within the inner self.

Over the span of 500 client sessions dealing with Mordrigal, to say it always looks one way or another would not be an accurate description. That is because what happens is this energy reads and defines the fear points and morphs to an identity inside the individual that reflects the fear that is unique to that person. For example, a client experiences a very traumatic event in their childhood, someone similar in nature to the perpetrator activates a memory related to that experience, an emotion. The Mordrigal energetic form then takes that emotion and turns the heat up, the volume so to speak, until the individual is steeped right back to the middle of the traumatic event. This is possibly a classic definition of how one might describe PTSD. Mordrigal has the necessary equipment to read and then exacerbate the emotion to the point of depression at the minimum to states of self-worthlessness and shame at the worst. The next chapter delves deeply into this phenomenon.

Consider that as human beings, we have more than one fear. We have more than one attachment to something. Think about all the things an individual has seen or experienced in life, what upsets them, distracts, and makes an impression on them. Those issues are all sitting in the back of the mind's consciousness. This is Mordrigal and how its energy is capable of victimizing an individual. Mordrigal uses the library within oneself to create things to confuse their life. For me, as a shaman, I cannot tell an individual, oh, it is definitely scales or shadows or demons or clowns or worms. It is whatever is in an individual's library that this energy pulls from, to wreak havoc in that person's life. It is a matter of defining what is not definable.

Again, it is to stress that this energetic form, called Mordrigal, comes from another source and uses a technology that, in my opinion, we have no idea how it works. What is identifiable, noted throughout this writing, is that there is a very concrete, non-varying, non-creative presentation on the chakra system that is routinely discernible to the trained eye. There exists a protocol that works in removing the most devastating aspects of this energetic form from the suffering individual. The deep Mordrigal energy plays out the specifics by accessing the individual's subconscious library, and that is where the full expression and the ability to address it in a healing way becomes tailored to the individual, and it is complicated at best.

CHAPTER 5

SOUL FRACTURES

Shame is LOUD!

Shame is the bottom line in suicide!

T
he concept of soul fracture is the heart of this book and the heart of the healing process for the kinds of devastation that occurs when an individual is wounded at a profound level. There is no way to sugarcoat this topic. It is here that the dip into a generally taboo, or at least to say the uncomfortable topic, has now arrived. There is a consistent thread within the database. Overwhelmingly the clients have suffered some level of sexual abuse, to one degree or another, sometime in their lifespan, in many cases, repeatedly in the lifetimes. Very often, when the client is asked about their ancestry, they will offer that yes, in fact, their mother or grandmother were abused, but the stories were never really open to discussion. In other words, the lineage carried a long history repeating itself generation after generation. The story that follows here is about Sweet Melissa and the journey that she has had to go through at a relatively very young age. The story, in her words, may at first seem almost unbelievable, however, I assure you that every aspect of what she shares here is true. I share this as the opening to this most difficult subject, a subject that is long overdue to come into the light of day. The bottom line in Sweet Melissa's story is the failure to hold a child in a safe environment, in a safe way, that has many dreadful consequences. Those consequences take the shape of the emotion of shame.

Sweet Melissa was suffering dissociation leading to a self-diagnosis of multiple personalities, more accurately two personalities. She knows there is only one part or personality that remembers what was happening, while the other part seemed to have no recollection of what was transpiring. Having known Sweet Melissa for some time and being with her in several different settings, it was quite interesting when we realized that I had little or no memory of her presence. This naturally gave us a place to begin our work together. She admitted that her invisibility has always been a prevalent condition, a condition that had existed throughout her life from early adolescence.

Once we initiated our working relationship, it quickly became apparent that she was experiencing the unwelcome dark energetic form of Mordrigal. As we began the journey into her early childhood development, overwhelmingly present was her experience of parental neglect, her not being held securely in the world at large, her home, or within the extended family. She reported early in the process that she had suffered from suicidal ideation throughout every day of her adult life.

Sweet Melissa was prepared to enter into a very deep working relationship, willing to mine the deepest aspects of the soul fractures she experienced throughout much of her life. There were early signs of relief from the severity of the invasion of Mordrigal; still, in every way, the journey has been long and hard. The following is a synopsis, in her words, telling her story:

> How does one explain a fog, a disconnection from
> life, when you feel like you are ripped into two
> parts? Every time I would start to see the light
> of day, I would be pulled back into the dark. It

was like being underwater and seeing the surface but unable to reach it. No one can hear you. I could see the surface but never reach it. I was alive but not connected to life. Whenever I was close, something would pull me back down.

I went through every kind of therapy there was, like talk therapy, equine, family constellation, medications of all kinds. Nothing could get me out of the separation from life. It was almost as though something was playing with me. I always knew when it happened, but I couldn't describe it. The more I would fight it, the harder it came on, putting me always back at square one, starting over, time after time. It was the cycle of always having to start over.

Initially, I thought it was alcohol that created separation and hopelessness. Once I stopped drinking, it all became even worse because before, I had the assumption that it was the alcohol. Ten years ago, I stopped drinking, and that is when the real battle began. That is when I realized something was disconnecting me from life. I was always suicidal, always a part of my adult life. While I was in psychiatric treatment, things got really bad. I was on thirty different drugs. Six different psychotropic drugs at the same time. These drugs destroyed my brain. My brain did not work anymore.

I left these treatment efforts one day when I woke

up and finally had clarity for some unknown reason. I decided to enter a graduate school program. During this time, daily, I had to be in the process of rebuilding my brain. I always have had an easy time learning, and it was here that again, I learned quickly, however, I couldn't get the learning out. For one year, every day, I had to retrain my brain!

The purpose of the drugs originally was to allow me to sleep. I had not slept for six months. I started on SSRIs and then anti-psychotic, anti-bi-polar drugs were added. Soon there were drugs to counter the side effects, with diagnosing side effects as symptoms of what I had. This is the norm in psychiatric settings. It was a complete miss by the psychiatric world, and unfortunately, I am not the exception. It is the worst possible experience you can have. They (the drugs) will kill the connection to life. This was abuse to a completely different level. Now six years later, I am starting to get to a point where I am stable from all of that treatment. These medications will cause you to go crazy. When asked if they (the psychiatric establishment) are aware, I answer, of course they are, there is money in the drugs and this kind of drug treatment.

I have been suicidal all of my life. These medications take away one's ability to reason, take away the ability to control, take away the fear of dying. They change the way you think, your ability to think. Death becomes something beautiful. One day I woke up and fired everyone, my psychiatrist, my treatment center, my relationships that were toxic and advantage-taking. Somehow, the lights went on, and I had clarity. I do not know what caused this; it just happened that there was one day when clarity arrived. I left the state, went to graduate school, and then began the long journey of rebuilding my brain back to some semblance of sanity. It has been a long healing journey the past six to seven years. My return to school was a high-level survival skill that I am so thankful to have been able to access.

I always felt that there were different parts of me, always some other part of self and that I had no idea of how to find that part. Once I actually saw my soul being split apart. After I was able to unload enough of the issues on top of me, that was when the torn part was discovered and brought forth. I was then able to begin the very deepest healing of my life, the merging of the torn part into my being. When we discussed sexual abuse, it was then when I saw the little girl in the kitchen, when I could see her, hear her … that is when I could see the rip, that is when I could heal it! It took months of working together to see her. I always knew but could never see her. It was my core wound.

After that moment, for the first time, I felt like one person. During my entire life, I have felt like I have been looking for something. After that moment of seeing, I knew that I could stop looking. I have stopped looking, and it is to now unfold the rest of my life.

Upon reflection, I was forced into working on these issues the past ten years, since I stopped drinking. I had panic attacks, felt I was going insane, and realized I had to either go deep and go through it— or go insane, meaning take my life. Until then, I had to fight to stay alive. The more fight, the stronger the energy. Once I surrendered, I could go deep. Just before our work, I realized it was the fighting. Always having to run. In this case, it would be to die. I have had, all of my life, daily conversations about dying. When this is happening, the voice of Spirit becomes a lot stronger. I realized if I killed myself, I would have to come back and go through this all again. My only option was to surrender completely. I had to go insane to reach out. I always do everything the hard way!

The lessons learned are larger than life.

A soul fracture involves a break in classically defined boundaries. One individual does not have the right or privilege to violate another individual, sexually or otherwise. For instance, healthy families have an honor code, meaning brothers and sisters don't have a right to violate each other, to have sex with each other. Mothers and fathers do not have the right to have sex with their children. Cousins don't beat up or rape other cousins. This is an honor code that has existed throughout time in healthy, nurturing communities and families. Parents should provide a safe environment for their children. When a violation of these deeply held boundaries occurs, we can barely comprehend the damage, the fracture that has occurred within one's energetic field. When a boundary has been broken, when a violation has occurred, it creates not just an injury to the physical body. The physical injuries heal fairly quickly. Bruises heal quickly. The infraction to the psychological and then energetic field will not heal as readily—that is until there is some type of intervention. Typically, as noted in Sweet Melissa's story, the psychological treatment could only go so far and, in fact, probably exacerbated the condition overall due to the overuse of medication. Then it was for the energetic intervention with the potential to reset and begin retrieving the broken parts of the self, the soul-remembering, beginning the journey back to wholeness. The energetic field begins to be strengthened back to a level where healthy functioning begins to emerge and then have a base from which to grow.

There is a difference between being cured and being healed. Curing occurs on just one level, usually the physical. Healing, in the best sense, occurs when the interventions take place on multiple levels, including the symbolic/psychological, the mythic or soul's journey, and then the pure energetic levels of understanding. If an individual has experienced a severe fracture to their essence and has not had the opportunity to work with it on all levels, it most likely has not been healed. One way to tell that healing has occurred concerning a particular event or experience is by discerning the degree of emotional charge the memory evokes in the person. A person holds body memory, emotional-psychological memory, as well as memories in the energetic field. An individual might feel intense energy around the memory imbedded within their field at any or all of these levels. The fractures manifest as the wound of shame where the dark, unwanted, and unwelcome energy of Mordrigal can enter. The energy of Mordrigal comes in where unhealed wounds reside. Mordrigal, as discussed previously, is an insidious energetic form that is capable of wreaking havoc within one's being to the point of self-destruction.

Throughout this chapter, a larger context is contemplated to understand what allows these dark unwelcome energetic forms to infiltrate the essences of certain individuals. Discussions include perspectives on understanding shame (David Hawkins, *Power vs. Force: The Hidden Determinants of Human Behavior* [Carlsbad, CA: Hay House, 2013]), learned helplessness, bullying, boundary issues, and then the aspects of free will as being pertinent within the overall context of healing.

David Hawkins, in his book *Power vs. Force: The Hidden Determinates of Human Behavior*, applies the rather complex concept of muscle testing to establish a type of hierarchy of levels of consciousness. Enlightenment is at the highest level, while shame resides at the very lowest. At this lowest level, the behavior around shame is proximate to death, banishment, isolation, and hallucinations. This description of shame affords, while dark and dire, an idea of why and how the energetic forms of Mordrigal find entry into one's energetic makeup.

Shame is the most pertinent concept because, as a society or culture, we seem hesitant to discuss shame openly. We are willing to see very notable personalities and individuals be removed from their field, permanently thrown out in response to their inappropriate sexual behavior. These removals, although quite appropriate, overlook the underlying causes of their behavior and worse, the underlying effects on their victims. The shame about what they perpetrated and the shame they caused to their victims is undeniable and requires a much deeper accounting. We seem to be saying, "We will get rid of them and all will be better." Some profound examples from the entertainment industry in the United States come to mind, such as Kevin Spacey, Harvey Weinstein, and Bill O'Reilly, just to name a few. Garrison Keillor, who was a very popular radio personality, was accused of inappropriate behavior. Whatever significant contributions these individuals made were sidetracked by throwing them out the door without any real attempt to understand the underlying factors that were at play. These examples are important because they represent the degree to which we essentially refuse to enter into a discussion about shame and how it manifests in an individual's reality. Specifically, there is an underlying shame that holds individuals within the devastating grasps of Mordrigal, wetiko, malignant egophrenia, or affliction.

LEARNED HELPLESSNESS

A very large percentage of clients who have the energy of Mordrigal also have experienced sexual trauma, as mentioned above. I am unable at this time to give a realistic estimate, yet I believe that it well exceeds 50 percent of my clients. One client, referred to as Nancy in the next chapter, described to me that being a victim of early sexual abuse created a condition she referred to as "learned helplessness." She found this term while researching childhood sexual abuse in the late 1980s while she was beginning to work through her healing process. Referring to that research, first written about by Martin E. P. Seligman in the late 1960s, she spoke about the statistical evidence that women who had experienced early sexual abuse were much more likely to be raped later in life. This was attributed to the victim projecting a sense of "learned helplessness," which the perpetrator was attuned to. As her understanding of the psychological, emotional, and somatically-held effects of childhood sexual abuse developed (she later became a clinician), she also grew to understand how early abuse affects developmental challenges and aspects of the personality.

All people have "parts of self" and an "inner conversation" between those parts. In cases of early abuse, the victim has a "part of self" that comes to identify with and mimic the abuser as a protective mechanism that makes the abuse more manageable. If an inner part of self reminds the victim of the perpetrator's point of view, the hope is that it may spare the victim some of the actual abuse. An example of this is that most perpetrators blame the victim for their actions with words such as "You are making me do this" and "It is all your fault." This becomes an inner voice that repeats this shaming and blaming, often referred to in psychological literature as the "inner critic." Nancy told me that through her experience, when the Mordrigal energy enters into the energy field to the degree that it seems to be talking to the victim, it perfectly assumes the role of the inner abuser that the victim feels powerless to stop, and the shaming and blaming can become intolerable.

Additionally, one of the ways that sexual abuse takes a toll is that it robs the victim of his or her sense of bodily integrity, making her feel that she has no control over her physical self. This is also an aspect of Mordrigal energy. Through the fracture in the energetic field, this energetic form can cause physical symptoms and to trigger somatically-held memories of past trauma to the body, increasing the victim's sense of helplessness and utter despair. Nancy described how, through all of this mimicking of already severe traumatic memories, the Mordrigal energy becomes "the ultimate sexual predator." It then suggests to the victim that there is no way out except to kill oneself. Simply put, this energetic form's goal is to cause the victim to commit suicide.

The feeling state of shame is capable of commanding a devastating toll on the human condition. Another client recently described the activation of the internalized abuser as paralyzing her. When she would become frightened, particularly by having a nightmare related to her early experiences of being molested, she would freeze, becoming paralyzed. She described lying in bed, unable to move even the tiniest muscle, and being frightened to move once the paralysis ended for fear of being in immense danger. As with several other victims of the energetic form, she claims that Mordrigal wanted her to kill herself, to feel there was no way out! This phenomenon of wanting one to commit suicide is not always the result of Mordrigal energy, however, it appears time and again as the desired endpoint in so many of the most severe and engaged situations.

Fight or flight (freeze more recently added) is a most basic mechanism that allowed humans to ascertain and prepare for an imminent danger on very short notice. The adrenal glands begin pumping cortisol and adrenaline throughout the body, and a state of heightened alertness results. Our current cultural ambiguity often can cause an individual to be in a perpetual state of being on guard, resulting in adrenal exhaustion. Such is the description offered above where the body became paralyzed by the somatic memory and would continue as such until an intervention occurred.

Many victims of sexual violence seek out the work and services of the shaman for healing. These clients have chronic problems forming positive, healthy relationships, seeming incapable of robustly surviving. As a shaman, it was necessary to come to an understanding of shame and the role it plays in creating soul fractures. A working theory about the devastating dynamics related to the way people act when shame is activated began to emerge. What happened was the beginning of seeing shame energetically. Soon shame began to manifest as energetically visible when working with clients during their energetic sessions. This was another profound turning point in the evolution of learning to work with the energetic form Mordrigal. The concept of shame and the devastation it leaves in its wake in the energetic field is of importance here. It is to bring forth this concept so that it can become a subject more forthrightly dealt with and put on the table. To call it out for exactly what it is—a soul fracture. Shame is the one absolute given in the massive epidemic of suicide that appears to be emerging at this time.

BULLYING AND SHAME

Recently, two children from the same high school killed themselves in the local community, here in Colorado. What has come out is that unknown to the parents, those two young people were being bullied. That probably includes the digital bullying that we know exists but is mostly un-seeable, meaning it is covert or stealth in nature. By the end of the week following the suicides, students walked out of the school in protest of bullying because the school administration was not dealing with it effectively (*Denver Post*).

Historically when the Columbine High School shootings happened, I was serving as a consultant with the State Department of Education, and Columbine was one of the districts that I was, on some level, accountable for. My bottom-line interpretation of that event was that bullying played a significant part in the incident. The high-end athletes were bullying the nerd group with whom the perpetrators identified. There are many ways to talk about what happened then, and through my research about this event, I concluded that, despite major denial, bullying was present and was not dealt with effectively. It is and was a closed situation in which people refused any truly open discussion, not unlike what we have seen when individuals are summarily dismissed from their positions with little, if any, discussion on a thoroughly explorative level. The attitude seems to have been to shove aside the perpetrators and have it over with. The wounds of Columbine continue to this day, with copycat phenomena at epidemic proportions, and little comprehensive healing other than for those individuals who have chosen to seek out the deepest forms of healing for themselves. Regarding both events of the two students taking their lives and then the Columbine school shooting, I suspect bullying, shame, and the Mordrigal energy referred to throughout this manuscript would have been at play in the broadest sense.

Further, at this time in the United States, we are experiencing an aggressive movement against the right of women to control their health, the opportunity to realize choices regarding decisions around pregnancy. In the most extreme situations, state legislatures are operating under the guidance of individuals who are legislating the end of the right to abortion, even in cases of rape and incest. In a sense, these men and women are indirect perpetrators themselves by participating in the act of creating legislated repression and reinforcing the wounds. It is impossible to bypass this regarding the subject of shame. The degree of devastation and shame that results from incest and rape is of great magnitude. The damage and the ability to mitigate the lasting effects for those who have been molested, raped, or are incest victims is incalculable. The impact can last a lifetime in most cases and the process to heal such acts of violation unending. The impact remains literally throughout one's life and may continue through the generations that follow. So many times, the factors around sexual violence reside heavily in the lineages of the individuals experiencing sexual violence.

Two situations of note involve individuals who are in their 60s and, through extensive treatment in the manner described in this book, still deal every day, on some level, with the everlasting imprints left behind from such boundary violations. 'In one situation, the individual knows the players in the family who participated in a most egregious pattern of incest. The second situation was described by my client as "murder by proxy," where, when we were able to track through her situation, her grandfather had raped his daughter, her mother, and then the grandfather committed suicide midway through the pregnancy that he caused. Guilt and shame? This scenario needed to be revealed for her to heal at the deepest level, thereby closing the trauma wound from in utero so that the Mordrigal energy could no longer enter her being through that soul fracture.

The total devastation and then the commitment to survival by both of these individuals has been most profound to witness. The elephant in the room needs to come forth. As unpleasant as it is, this energy does need to be brought out into the open. We can no longer afford to sit idly by or dance around these subjects. The time has come if we want to heal as individuals. The degree of inhumanity that exists, perhaps since the beginning of time, is literally and in every respect unacceptable, untenable, and egregious by any definition one might want to consider.

Mordrigal energy can come in through the energetic field of damage left behind in a victim of bullying. Referring to students who have killed themselves, it is possible to draw a line from suicide to being bullied. It would suggest that two functions are going on with Mordrigal. First of all, the individuals that kill themselves had a soul fracture or family fracture of some kind in their energetic field. That fracture could have come ancestrally and manifested over time.

Second, the other side of that coin is that there may be some driving force in the bully that has pushed him or her to be a perpetrator. Why do people commit incest? Why do people rape other people? Why are these violations taking place at such a level, with such frequency? This is not to excuse this behavior, only to open a possible avenue to a greater beginning of the healing process. Perpetrators are not healthy individuals either.

Mordrigal is an energetic bully. It would seemingly meet

every definition of a bully that exists. Making this significant link, we can then identify how to heal the devastation this energetic form leaves behind. The major component within the phenomena presented here is the soul fracture. Calling it anything less is softening the reality that has occurred. It is a fracture of the integrity which we know exists within the codes of ethical, moral behavior. Soul fractures may also manifest as guilt, abandonment, and even archetypal syndromes because of their overwhelming presence throughout all societies, core values, and even to the greatest and worst degree, in the cultures that practice, for example, female genital mutilation (FGM).

THE IMPORTANCE OF BOUNDARIES

First, there is a violation of long-accepted classically defined boundaries. Experiencing a soul fracture via or through a violation of boundary, then yields to the other side of the coin the ability to establish healthy boundaries that will allow for healing to take place. Shame makes it very difficult to establish these healthy boundaries. The function of shame is generally impervious to insight-oriented therapy or treatment. It tends to not work well in consideration of deep healing. Society at large, the field of education, and specifically the field of psychology have seemingly often been stumped with how to heal the wounds that come from the kinds of sexual violations, in particular, that individuals referred to here have experienced. Part of it is that if an individual is raped, he or she would likely have PTSD in the form of shamefulness. Another way to speak to the emotional phenomena surrounding these levels of boundary violations includes guilt, abandonment, and isolation.

Recent alternative approaches utilized in the trauma field

include EMDR, or eye movement desensitization and reprocessing, developed by Francine Shapiro as a student in 1987, "parts work" or ego-state intervention strategies developed by Richard Schwartz; as well as somatic memory work developed and defined by Peter Levine.

If shame is essentially impervious to being healed through talking about it, then one thing that becomes very important for the victim is the setting of effective boundaries. It is a type of oxymoron to utilize the same ingredient that caused the infraction in the first place as the means to heal. Yet, part of the process of getting through shame is to set boundaries and to honor those boundaries and not allow them to be violated. For example, the person may experience a feeling of being sick inside, glum, and disoriented when confronted with a perpetrator or even anyone who reminds them of any aspect of their perpetrator. The person loses touch with their "self," not hearing their Song of the Soul. That is prime territory to set a boundary and say, "Hey, I'm not going to be around that person anymore. Every time I am, I get this feeling. I don't know what it is. I can't especially put words to it, but it makes me feel less than myself. I cannot be around that person." An appropriate response to that is not to keep stepping through the same experience time after time. The healthy, appropriate response is to set the boundary, to say, even as painful as it may be, "I'm not going to have anything more to do with this situation until I can heal this within myself."

Such boundary-setting is very important. Clients often speak about a parent who they say they have not talked to in several years. Or perhaps say they just saw that parent earlier that day and feel lousy. One way to respond to that is to reframe the issue as a setting of boundaries, healthy boundaries. When they proceed through the healing process successfully, they may be able to spend time with that individual. It is the boundary that allows for the healing to take place. The process of boundary-setting begins opening the healing process around the fracture within the soul. It sometimes takes a full lifetime to find this inner strength. Other times, it may be a matter of plunging right back into the circumstance that caused the fracture, however, with firm boundaries, which then allows for a structure for the healing to take place.

An example is a client I refer to as Ms. Sharp. She started her working relationship with me, asking for her home to be cleared of very negative energy. As our working relationship emerged, it became clear that she was experiencing the phenomena of the unwelcome energetic form referred to here as Mordrigal. She was isolated from her work, her home, her community, and—most devastatingly to her—specifically her children. The course of treatment included her return back to the environment she was expelled from and, therefore, isolated, to reenter to regain the relationship with her children. It was daring, and yet, it was with newfound boundaries that allowed her to reenter and confront the monster in the belly of the beast. Here the point is that the healing of the specific family relationship mattered, not so much the many other aspects of the situation. Each extended relationship was important, though it was the relationship to her children that called out so strongly, that with healthy boundaries, she was able to begin the re-entry process back into her world.

Several different types of boundaries help maintain a healthy sense of self. The first boundary is a physical boundary. A physical boundary, different for every individual, may be if someone is standing inside your physical space and you feel uncomfortable. You feel invaded. For some people, their physical boundary is a foot; for others, it may be three feet. Every person's physical boundary is different, but if somebody, depending on your relationship with them, is standing too close inside your comfort zone, you may feel like your boundaries are being violated.

Further, refusing to be in someone's presence is certainly an acceptable boundary. Ms. Sharp's total isolation was also, in a sense, a type of boundary where she refused to allow herself any further abuse within certain aspects of her situation. She referred to her survival during this period as commandeering "the army of her passivity." She played mindless computer games, yet she is (and was) a highly acclaimed intellectual in the life from which she had become isolated.

There are emotional boundaries. People can have an emotional boundary that is set, and if someone breaks that boundary or emotional agreement, one again might feel violated. We see it inside relationships where somebody breaks or violates an emotional commitment. Someone may have a friendship, and the other person perceives it differently. Healthy family boundaries may include that just because you are family doesn't mean you have 100 percent access to that individual's life. Think of the parent who's looking through the backpacks of their children all the time, looking through the drawers, emails, and texts, looking to find out about the private life of a family member, whether it's a child, a wife, or a significant other. It is a violation of privacy and the boundaries associated with the privacy of information.

It is also possible to see violations of people's time as boundaries. Sometimes you see this with colleagues or friends who show up or call unannounced or interrupt you while you're working. You tell them you're busy, yet they are slow to leave or refuse to get off the phone. That is violating boundaries of time and workspace. While some of the boundaries are not as invasive or as significantly emotionally damaging as others, they still represent ways in which one human being can disrespect or violate another human being.

Then there are more intimate boundaries, both physical and verbal, that can be violated. If it is among family members, the damage is more significant than if it was a stranger. If you're sixteen years old and a stranger says, "You have nice-looking breasts," it's not as damaging as if you are sixteen years old, and your dad says, "Your breasts look nice." Who the perpetrator is can enhance the significance of the boundary violation.

MORE ON BULLIES AND THE BULLIED

Bullies violate boundaries: emotional, verbal, and/or physical boundaries. Frequently, what is so damaging is that an individual may never know when a bully is going to strike. They show up in an unexpected way and ambush. It puts the victims of bullies in a constant state of fear and anxiety. The bullied are in a heightened, agitated fear state, and that becomes constant. This can evolve into shame. They are tied together. Being bullied, shame, suicidality, and soul fractures are all tied together by seeming almost always to involve boundary violations.

Everyone's boundary lines are different. It is an intrusion or an invasion. An invasion is intentional; an intrusion can be accidental. Often, people may interfere with our boundaries without knowing it. Let's say you are with someone, and they are standing too close to you. They have intruded on your boundaries, but they did not necessarily invade you. You step away because you are uncomfortable. Perhaps someone tells you something you do not want to know. People may say "TMI" or too much information. Those are more like boundary intrusions. Someone might be more forthcoming with their energy than you are comfortable with.

In our societies at large, in the collective, we have bullies. White supremacists who will put swastikas on a Jewish headstone are bullies, among other things. They create an invasion of a cultural boundary. Someone who would drive a car into a crowd in Charlottesville, or a truck into a crowd in Nice, France, is someone committing a boundary invasion that is off the charts. That is exponentially greater than anything we may want to consider; however, it might be worth thinking about what would drive that person to do that. According to Hawkins, hate and anxiety are conditions rather than emotions. Shame, fear, and anger register as very low-frequency emotions. It is shame, fear, and anger that are the most significant issues here. Bullying is a matter of fracturing a person's soul. Shame may well function as a common denominator, such that for those people who feel shame, some end up being victimized, and some who feel rage become bullies. Imagine two people who both grew up in the same type of environment. There is not always a way to tell, energetically, which way a person could go. Some people punish themselves while others become punishers. What's very important is some people overcome these circumstances and achieve varying levels of healing, often depending on their resources. Some individuals internalize the shame they live with by going within and withdrawing so far away to the point of just wanting to leave. Other people who we might call the rage mongers become perpetrators, externalizing their shame. They have so much rage and anger that they go to the other extreme and become that energy.

People have the opportunity to choose as an adult who they want to be in this world. At that crossroad, a person may sometimes choose by not choosing, yet again, they are choosing, only unconsciously. Assuming a victim archetype in life will then create a situation where everything will victimize that individual. Being a victim as a child is one thing, but now, as an adult, there is a chance to choose differently. Is one going to go ahead and reaffirm the victim experience or the archetype of victimization? Every event in life victimizes the individual. In that case, it may seem that one is victimized anywhere and everywhere. In a like manner, if people adopt a survival type of approach to life, they will always be surviving something in their life because they are in that archetype by choice.

Individuals can also say they are never going to let anyone hurt them in the same way they experienced earlier in life. The only way to know that it is not going to happen is if they become the ones perpetrating the hurt. They adopt the perpetrator archetype in their life and become the bullies. "My family violated my boundaries, pushed me around, were aggressive to me. I'm going to adopt being a perpetrator now, so no can mess with me." They might live their whole life perpetrating, yet never realizing or verbalizing any of those decisions on a conscious level.

The point is, we have these choice points in our lives, and we always play a role. Because a person has soul fractures like those described in this chapter does not mean they are doomed to this archetypal role for the rest of their life. It is not their destiny to always be a victim, nor is it to always be a perpetrator, nor to always be in survival mode. It is possible to choose to be a healed, unique self-realized "Soul Self." A person can go to their highest self, listen to the Song of the Soul identity, and transcend beyond these perpetrator, survivor, victim, archetypal roles. On some level, it is a person's choice.

These kinds of experiences in life are archetypal. They evolve into a manner of interacting that falls into universal patterns or archetypes. An archetype reflects a pattern that can be found across all cultures. Unconsciously, these archetypal patterns become prevalent in the individual's way of interacting in the world. Without realizing it, they have successfully become an actor in the archetypal pattern related to the victim, the perpetrator, or the survivor. Then, enter Mordrigal's special sauce. This energetic form accesses your entire subconscious as its own library. That sauce enhances and amplifies the behavior related to the pattern. Mordrigal did not make people bullies. Individuals choose consciously to behave in certain ways. "Hey, I'm going to go up to that kid and throw him in a locker," "I'm going to post damaging information about someone on social media because I think it's funny, or cool." These are human beings that are operating on a free-will choice, as the universe has designated all of us as human beings to have a free-will choice to operate in an archetypal pattern of their choice. They are choosing to be a perpetrator. They are choosing to do those activities. There is not a dark energy forcing them to do that. Enter again, the learned helplessness. As adults, enter into the crossroad of choice and free will.

CHAPTER 6

A TURN TO HEALING

P lease, here lies an invitation to come onto this stage now and join this effort of emphasizing light over dark forces. It is the journey to a consciousness of who we are and how we can be free from the forces emanating from the dark side of things. Now it is the time to turn to heal.

I have had many people tell me that it is to love this energetic form to relieve its most devastating qualities. I have churned on this thought over a great period of time. The reason is that it is quite difficult to find any evidence regarding this dark energetic form that is positive. Specifically, the writer, Paul Levy, suggests that the energy of wetiko causes one to be called to greater healing. Similarly, he also applies that concept to the greater societal culture. While this may have some truth to it, certainly and this suggestion does not excuse, on any level, this entity's most devastating qualities and manifestations.

This energetic form, at the most extreme, appears to delight in persuading individuals that they are unworthy of being in this world at all. An entity that would ultimately suggest hopelessness, to the point of taking one's own life at the most extreme, is hardly worthy of any degree of respect. Likewise, regarding the larger or greater societal culture and the kinds of darkness prevailing in the world today, thinking that there is a clarion call to healing may be more important than we could ever imagine. There is a requirement here to be bold, firm, and unanswered in the pursuit of peace and the deterrence of the prevailing darkness within humanity.

Simone Weil speaks to the concept of affliction, having written during the 1920s and 30s as a condition that "freezes and hardens the soul with scorn, disgust, self-hatred, guilt, and defilement." She suggests that it is necessary to have both the dark malheur and light love to exist in this world. Again, no doubt this is true, and yet, it is a challenge to accept the egregiousness of the dark Mordrigal energetic form, the affliction, the wetiko.

A colleague has suggested it is a manner of forgiving this energy, not holding any emotion toward it at all, and then it will have no purchase, no hold. After giving a talk regarding this subject, another colleague came to me and said: "You just have to love this 'entity,' otherwise it will not give way." I came to a deep understanding of a recent teaching engagement that what it meant when the statement is made to love this energetic form is really to love and care for oneself. Yet another client declared recently that any aspect of self-nourishment would cause this energetic form to lose interest, as its deepest quest is in self-destruction. When one cares for themselves, Mordrigal tends to be much less interested. More directly, the individual, with self-care, becomes notably less available to the energetic form of Mordrigal.

I confess that I have gained the greatest insights into this energetic form through working with some of the most severe situations imaginable. However, it is to say that the overall leap is the learning that has impacted all client interventions, no matter what level of issues they present. I am always immensely grateful when a client enters my office, and they are not a victim of this energetic form of Mordrigal. It is a validation that tells me—vindicates me—that I am not projecting my issues onto the clients. Sometimes, in the past, I have worried that I was creating an energetic form. I would liken it to when an individual has a severe allergy, tends to that allergy with great discipline, and then stops their careful discipline thinking that it is all in their head. Then when exposed to the allergen, suddenly, they are reminded of the reality by again experiencing a reaction, sometimes severe in nature.

The point being, it is not the most severe clients, but rather the learnings and generalizations that have been attained by working with the most extreme situations. The importance is to recognize how these learned skills and understandings apply broadly to the overall population. This interest area and effort are to bring this malevolent energetic form to the light, the dazzling light of day, awareness, and consciousness. Where there is dark, there is light. They go hand in hand. It is always the same: it is to seek balance.

The goal is to create a format where this information comes forth and can be considered for a full and robust dialogue, ideally in a public forum of whatever format might become available. This energetic form has been and is creating havoc in our world for untold numbers of people. It seems this energy is happy to destroy people's well-being, their self-concept, and self-worth in so many situations. It is time now that we begin to transcend this energy as a whole community. It is now a call that community is our most important tool to combat the devastation of isolation. The challenge here is just short of impossible, though proposed here is to step toward and realize an optimistic posture. Our nature as human beings contains endless amounts of resilience when called upon. Let us now consider opening our hearts to that most fundamental aspect of human nature.

My clients have made statements such as: "I felt as though I was in a chest wrapped in chains at the bottom of the ocean," "I felt ejected out of the cosmos," "My voice was taken away— muzzled," "The first attack was at my heart and left breast. It squeezed my heart, trying to destroy it, pressuring it until I thought it would explode."

This is a species of energy that we have been discussing. This energy binds with one's self-language, inner dialogue, and then turns it against the individual. This energetic species counts on isolation so much so that while attacking, an individual's life is threatened, and the individual is afraid to tell anyone for fear that they will be diagnosed with a major psychological illness. This has been a consistent pattern throughout all of my experience with this energetic form. For instance, right now, if a reader has experienced any of the manifestations presented here and throughout this book, that person might feel relieved to see that others have experienced these very same symptoms. If the reader, on the other hand, has no familiarity with any of the issues and topics presented here, then it is possible one might say this whole discussion is somewhat crazy and sounds like a case of insanity.

I want to share that as I have compiled the data represented here, I have withstood a very long period of finding very few individuals that I could discuss this with, my own isolation. Within the case histories that I have accumulated over the past fifteen years, well-meaning families and physicians have placed their clients and loved ones in psychiatric hospitals, for lack of knowing what malady was confronting their loved one, or their client. That is a result of not knowing what to do on their behalf. Then, the situation would be further exacerbated with heavy psychotropic drug therapy, which would help to perhaps suppress and dull the active self-destructive expressions, but unfortunately, further isolate and alienate the individual at a time when the exact opposite was needed.

Some of the information presented here, such as Sweet Melissa's intense life story, may appear as an indictment of the psychological field. That is not the intent. Hopefully, most of this information can be held as an invitation to join in a broader discussion of the deeper dynamics of healing at the soul level. This aspect of healing is not something to be feared, as the soul is filled with love and hope, as in the metaphor of the Song of the Soul. We all carry innately the capacity to love and, even more important, the need to be loved. When fear becomes operational, then that aspect of the human soul is so often lost. It is the loving nature that needs to be nurtured. Fear is preventative to healing in so very many situations.

I would like to bring forward again the concept of a pyramid of degrees of severity. At the lightest level, it has been possible to remedy the existence of Mordrigal within one energetic session. Then as the pyramid descends, there has been a group of clients who have experienced a complete cleansing from this energetic form within five to six energetic healing sessions. Add another level, where clients who have attempted the work for one to two sessions for whatever reason have abandoned the effort, perhaps because that was enough to heal, or perhaps the will was not there to continue with the long journey. The next category, proceeding down the pyramid, would be those who have experienced ten to twenty sessions with varying degrees of success. Once we have exceeded twenty sessions, it could then be estimated that those clients at the bottom of the pyramid require an open-ended number of sessions to clear themselves. Thus, it is to say that dealing with this energetic form is quite challenging and quite variable in its presentation and resolution. The longer this energetic form exists untreated, the greater the difficulty in removing it successfully.

I would like to share some additional experiences and insights gained with clients who have experienced this energetic form called Mordrigal. Nancy Portland was a client who came to me thinking about either harming herself or someone near and dear to her. She was preparing to come and meet directly with me, even though it required traveling a considerable distance. Just before her planned arrival, she admitted herself to a psych hospital because she needed to protect the harming instinct that was present in the form of hurting herself, her significant other, and her most loved puppy dog. When she was released from the hospital, this was the beginning of a long and rich relationship extending the learning about removing this energetic form and working to keep it at arm's length distance at a minimum, and ideally off of her altogether. In a nutshell, the seriousness of her situation was that she was violated at the point of conception, through the misbehavior of one of her significant family member. This resulted in a lifelong effort to seek healing, and remedy of the everlasting pain associated was such a violation of boundary. The pain associated with this is what was referred to in the last chapter regarding family fractures—violations of the boundaries that healthy families follow innately.

Her situation had a seemingly firm beginning when one of her clients committed suicide. Nancy Portland was a therapist at the time. It is her belief that her client had the energetic form of Mordrigal at the time of his death. She states that it was at this point when the Mordrigal energetic form entered onto and into her being. At the beginning, it appeared as a benevolent energy offering her great enlightenment, until the day arrived when she began to realize the true malicious nature of what had landed on her and consumed her psyche.

The journey of healing for Nancy has been long and arduous, requiring the very deepest of healing of those wounds that were sustained prenatally. Just by this description alone, it may be easier for the reader to understand that there is no easy way to describe and delve into this subject of sexual violation. It is far more pervasive than anything I had ever imagined. In these most severe situations, the healing process requires a profound effort. In an era when there is a questioning of a woman's right to control her body, it is most unfortunate that there is truly a lack of understanding of the profound impact that sexual molestation, rape, and incest have in an everlasting manner on their victims. I, along with any number of my clients, can speak in depth to the profound magnitude of the damage that is done to one's psychic, spiritual, and physical well-being by these acts of sexual violence.

It is one thing to celebrate life from conception. It is quite another issue when the newcomer is conceived and born under severely hostile and brutal circumstances. There appears to be a profound failure to understand any number of issues surrounding the current and ongoing discussions pertaining to the issue of abortion. To put it plainly, the individuals aggressively legislating governmental restrictions are, one more time, presenting themselves as indirect perpetrators and violators of the soul, the Song of the Soul. This point, as a writer, reflecting on the immense amount of data that I hold surrounding this subject, my silence is not maintainable! It is at least the individual's right to choose. I am not at all saying that any of the situations herein described would have been appropriate to such a choice as abortion, however certainly a decision by the victim of sexual violence should and must be afforded the opportunity to make their own decisions regarding something as momentous of an occasion as bringing life into this world.

Nancy's journey has revolved around her life's work of healing from the very earliest of family fracture imaginable. She was tricked most dramatically by this energetic form. She was naively going along in life when the energy of Mordrigal landed with both feet fully upon her complete and total makeup, her complete and total being.

Her situation is one where the severity of the boundary intrusion was such that it was repeated many times throughout her childhood, and perhaps into her adulthood to some degree. She has experienced two psych hospitalizations, one actual suicide attempt, and battles with Mordrigal too numerous to list, sometimes appearing unending. Her perseverance has been astounding, and her knowledge that the impact from the energetic form is real and yet not residing within her psychic makeup is ever so important. In other words, she has understood that there has been this external entry separate from her being.

My first contact with her began in 2015, particularly as the protocol was unfolding. It was the depth of the work with Nancy that has allowed very significant insights into the overall treatment of this energetic form. I went through stages of literally trying every possible type of intervention. It is through these efforts that I learned the strategy of intervention, the importance of persistence, perseverance, and being reliably and consistently available. This requires a willingness to surpass in very certain ways some of the traditional boundaries found in Western medicine's fondest paradigms. It is about humility and meeting one's clients on a fundamentally equal and nonjudgmental platform. It is always the client's reality that the shamanic practitioner is dealing with, not the practitioner's reality, such as is found in the most basic aspects of judgementalism.

I cannot imagine writing about Mordrigal without mention of Nancy. When one experiences such great pain, it is not uncommon for that pain to express itself, sublimate, into overt expression through some aspect of the arts. There is no exception here. The degree of pain experienced by Ms. Portland is expressed through various aspects of art, which she asked that I not reveal at this time. However, the brilliance being expressed throughout her life in these other forums is spectacular. The prices that are paid by the artistic greats are something to behold.

Now enter Remy, who lives in one of our most rural states west of the Mississippi River. She was raised on a farm and spent most of her adult life married and raising three boys, also on a farm. She left the farm and her family in fear for her life. The journey for Remy has also been one of great effort, persistence, and tenacity to continue surviving. Her survival has been a testimony of the resilience held in our human nature. We entered into a working relationship that has continued over several years. She always arranged for an appointment when she was in very severe discomfort.

In her 60s, Remy consistently stated that she had suffered a "murder by proxy" that was unknown to her, even why she would make such a statement. As we delved into the depths of her situation growing up, it was one day when we were able to go significantly deeper into her lineage. She described with great acuity her early childhood as being mostly disheveled and disconnected. It is here where the metaphor of the onion and the layers being peeled back applies. Layer after layer had been worked with until finally, in one particular session, it became available to see exactly what had happened during her prenatal development. Her grandfather had raped his daughter, her mother, and then the grandfather committed suicide midway through the pregnancy that he caused. She was aware of the suicide of her grandfather, though not the impregnation of her mother by her mother's father. Guilt and shame? It was mandatory, unavoidable in the overall healing scenario, that this information is revealed for her to heal at the deepest level. It was at this point in her healing journey that the closing of this traumatic wound, the suicide of her grandfather, be reckoned with. It was the wound in utero that the Mordrigal energy entered her through and which had to be closed, had to be healed by bringing the information to the light of day. This was the event, the information that began the ending of the intrusion into her being, her soul being, where Mordrigal could no longer enter her psyche. It was here that I learned the extraordinary importance of finding the core issue and bringing it forth in a way that consummates the healing process. Game over for Mordrigal.

In a somewhat like manner, Ms. Sharp has also taught me many lessons as this protocol has evolved. Again, it is in the depth of pain that sometimes the most extraordinary accomplishments occur. Ms. Sharp was most articulate upon our meeting, expressing that she was so tired of hearing from healers that all she had to do was honor the energy, build an altar, and love it away. Her statement most profoundly was that she was sick of hearing about "butterflies and rainbows." She was experiencing complete isolation from her world, her society, her culture, and, most significantly, her family. When she was able to first experience the feeling of not having this energetic form on her or in her, even briefly, she spoke to this as the first time she was able to feel real hope, calling it "substantiated hope." That term has stayed with me throughout all of this work. Ms. Sharp articulated the profound reality that there are very severe conditions that typically are not dealt with in the overall energetic healing literature.

Ms. Sharp is the person who introduced me to the works of Simone Weil. In that work, Weil introduces the idea of metaxu, which is essentially a bridging concept where bridges are built for the individual back into life as they have known it. This was realized on one very major level by working to clear the energy in her home, which included interacting and bridging her back toward some normalcy with her family. This happened following very intense session work between the two of us. Ms. Sharp felt that even her appearance had been altered by the Mordrigal energy. Through a significant part of her healing, it was recommended to her that she cover her mirrors so as not to reactivate the strength with which the Mordrigal energetic form had invaded and harassed her. Ms. Sharp's journey has been arduous and strenuous in so many ways. In particular, she was willing to go directly back into the center of the breakdown in her relationships and begin rebuilding herself and her relations to her children. She entered with boundaries and a clear understanding of who and what she is all about. It is with great regard that I share even the smallest aspect of her journey in slaying the monster revealed to her as Mordrigal. She has been successful in returning to her writing career.

The cases shared here are with the highest regard and reflect the most earnest energetic commitments to reaching the healed state by all parties involved.

CHAPTER 7

THE MORDRIGAL
PROTOCOL

The short take on this chapter is that once the overlay (the circuit breaker concept) is removed from the energetic body of the client, then the shamanic intervention leading to the deepest healing can begin to take place.

It may be perceived that I am addressing the practitioner alone in this chapter. I would like to clarify that I believe it is appropriate for the client to be thoroughly aware of exactly what is happening as well. I have little hesitation in placing this information in a broad format for all to see and understand. The context for this treatment protocol has typically been held with a certain degree of caution, such as stating to students that they are being trained in a manner surrounded by a deep context to frame this protocol. However, at this point, given that the reader has pursued the full detail in this writing as the context for this instruction, I am trusting that a more complete understanding of what is being presented here is in place.

Additionally, in that a great deal of the work described herein has taken place in remote sessions, there is a certain comfort level for me in describing this protocol in more detail here. Since there is not a face-to-face interaction in remote session work, only the auditory ear-to-ear contact, it is appropriate to give a reasonably detailed verbal description of what is taking place. This then facilitates the client to be able to visualize the treatment. Thus, the detailed description that follows is quite similar to how I would choose to approach the client.

This chapter delves deeply into the process of shamanic treatment, with particular emphasis on the removal of energies associated with the Mordrigal energetic form. A session typically begins the same for all clients, that of observing the energetic functioning of their chakra system. Depending on a practitioner's training, that may be accomplished in any number of ways. The single most important point: It is not just one look, but the repeated observation of the chakra functioning where significant and important diagnostic information is attained.

The key point here is that there is a typical kind of presentation where one or more of the chakras are holding the energy the client has entered the session with. The second condition is where a presentation deviates significantly, such as the chakra system is presenting highly unusual patterns. As mentioned previously, it is where all seven chakras are functioning in the same way, and then the next pass over all seven, they are all functioning oppositely, with yet a third pass, where again all seven chakras are acting in still a third way. To state it plainly, this is not the expected pattern, and this way indicates the presence of something operating other than the individual's chakra system. There is an overlay present. This is the most fundamental key to the diagnostic evaluation of the Chakra Operating System, the COS, if you will, not unlike your phone or computer operating system.

All practitioners may not observe the same pattern, however, at a minimum, they should be keying in on the fact that the presentation is not normal, as in the pattern is not similar to what their training has indicated to be typical. This is the first indicator that something is not correct in an overall sense. Let's lay some groundwork here for the "seeing" endeavor ahead.

The shamanic practitioner looks for several forms of energetic attachments on individuals, usually as an initial type of intake look at their client. Traditionally, there was identification of three types of intrusive energetic form attachments and methods for extraction, as noted in chapter 3. The first would be a fluid type of attachment, reflecting any number of possibilities as to what that might be, all the way from the energy of a passerby to the energy of someone close to the individual.

The second type of attachment referred to is a crystallized form attached to the physical body. Theoretically, crystallized because it was a physical wound experienced in times past and that same wounding would be repeated. Think of the statement where one says, "I feel like I was stabbed in the back." The practitioner might say here that perhaps one was stabbed in the back sometime in the past, including other lifetimes, and the result is an actual physical manifestation because that wounding has happened repeatedly so often that it manifested in an almost palatable crystallized energetic form. This is where the practitioner might also identify a cord that could be connected to their client. A cord may be seen as a connection to another individual or even a concept that is held so strongly that it manifests literally as a cord. Every tradition or mystery school has a version of a way to cut cords successfully, and again, not necessarily one better or more appropriate than another. The sensing of this category of energetic attachment is done with the seer's sensitivity in whatever modality is a particular strength for that specific practitioner.

The third area of energetic form extraction is removing the deepest of wounds by traveling in circular time to the events and aspects of the traumas that serve as the true level where soul fractures live. In this writing, it is not appropriate to go into a deep explanation because these are techniques that require very significant training. Refer back to Remy and the discovery of her "murder by proxy" and how that was healed. It was through this methodology which requires the eyes and skills of the mature and well-trained shamanic practitioner.

Referring back to the story of Sweet Melissa in chapter 5, I would like to describe a form of crystallized, energetic attachment that was preventing her healing from being realized. When we began her treatment, once seeing the presence of Mordrigal, I moved directly into the protocol of removing its energetic representation. This involved removing the surface overlay as described in chapter 4, and then the control centers, or sending/receiving units. Soon it became apparent that she had some kind of a gigantic boulder-like energetic attachment sitting on her torso, pressing the life out of her. This boulder needed something equivalent to dynamite to break it apart and remove it from her. The image I had was that it was similar to when a boulder randomly falls down a mountainside and lands in the middle of the road, blocking the road from all further traffic. One can only hope that they are not accidentally under it by truly being in the wrong place at the wrong time. The only remedy, depending on the size, as was the case of this recent event when a boulder landed in the middle of the road, was for the highway department to use dynamite to blow it to pieces and begin the process of removal. This happened recently and was reported in the local, statewide newspaper. It was estimated that the boulder weighed over 100 tons.

Literally, for Sweet Melissa, the weight and breadth of the boulder sitting on her torso spanned from her second chakra through to her sixth chakra. In all of the clients I have ever worked with, never have I observed such an enormous weight being carried by any one individual. It turns out that I suspect this was the weight of a long lineage going back many generations. The weight of this noble lineage was as strong in every dimension as one could conjure up in their wildest imagination.

I share this description because several very important dimensions are represented here. The first and most important is that Sweet Melissa was ready to deal with this major blocking in her life. She had worked endlessly on all of the surrounding issues, coming at them from every possible strategy and therapeutic intervention one can find. Yet, seeing this boulder, ever so present and yet so unseeable, it was perhaps only now that it finally became available to be worked with.

The second very important dimension is that until that boulder was removed, almost all other interventions were not likely to be profitable. Again, this boulder-like block was only seeable once the overlay and the sending/receiving units were removed. While all of the efforts at healing accumulated in a way to bring her to the point of our work together, it was the immense frustration she was experiencing in the denial of her real healing that was making her life unbearable.

The point here is that surface issues must be dealt with before all other work. No matter how majestic and magical any interventions might be, no matter how great the intention of both the client and the clinician, until the surface issues are dealt with, no further healing can or will take place. That is the same principle with having necessarily to deal with the overlay and sending/receiving unit concepts associated with the Mordrigal energetic form.

The metaphor of the childhood game of pick-up sticks may help to demonstrate the importance of removing the easily accessed items before entering into the most delicate operation of untangling the issues (or sticks) from the center. Another metaphor is how peeling the layers of an onion is similar to peeling down through the many issues one faces and carries throughout their life. As one layer is peeled off, the next layer then becomes available to be worked on. In Sweet Melissa's situation, it may be that all of the frustrating work she had engaged in finally led her to bring forth the biggest barrier she faced and needed to deal with.

There was nothing lightweight about the 100-kilo boulder sitting on Sweet Melissa's body, no pun intended. The boulder analogy is strictly metaphorical. Regarding Mordrigal, Sweet Melissa had every aspect of this dark, unwanted, unwelcome energetic form on her and within her. The boulder could not be seen until the overlay was removed from her. The phenomenon here is that when Mordrigal enters, the overt presence of it is most dramatic in that it breaks the connection between an individual's physical body and their Song of the Soul. Sweet Melissa, for some unknown amount of time, has been walking in the world without the benefit of being connected to her higher self. That was additionally complicated by this boulder, for lack of a better description, right underneath the overlay. Sweet Melissa's situation is rather extreme, yet she had the financial resources necessary to travel the path to healing. She walks in the world of a double-edged sword. The circumstances she was raised in caused many of her troubles, and it is likewise her circumstances that allow her to find her way to the healed self, to be able to find her Song of the Soul.

It is here that I want to press the case for knowing there is hope. There is a protocol. It is an evolving protocol for intervening with the darkness prevailing at this time. This effort here is truly about bringing the Dark to the Light. It is about outing Mordrigal, who has been having free rein with its insidious tactics.

It is rather difficult to work with the energy of Mordrigal on one's own. That is because if you have that overlay, you're not as likely to be able to see it, and you're not as likely to be able to remove it. It is close to an impossibility. I think this is where I learned never to trust intuitively that I know that Mordrigal is on a client or within a client. I will never say definitively that Mordrigal is present until I've used the pendulum, until I've gone through that process of assessment. I never second-guess the presence of the Mordrigal energetic form, ever.

The intervention then is where the healing work begins to take place. One more time, what is conceptually enormously important is that if this energetic form is present and you fail to see or deal with it, your efforts in all other avenues will be less than productive, if at all.

A practitioner might say to themselves, for instance, "I am suspicious or pretty sure that the chakra pattern I am seeing does not fit anything I have seen before. I am not sure what to do, yet I am just going to go ahead and proceed as if everything is as usual." The point here is a line of thinking that will not work, as any further efforts will be for naught. It is not going to have any impact whatsoever because, again, back to the pick-up sticks, you have to get things off the surface before you can go and do the deeper work. This is fundamentally the starting point with any intervention, the removal of issues resting and appearing on the surface level of the client.

For Sweet Melissa, the first three sessions were entirely involved with the removal of the overlay and control units, and then this boulder-like form covering five of her seven chakras. It is no wonder that only incrementally minimal progress had been made on her healing behalf up to the point of the removal of this boulder-like energetic form.

Part of any intervention is looking and listening diagnostically to what is being said and seen. It is looking for patterns in both language and physical mannerisms. When we see a person who has a tic—a certain behavior that is repeating—that behavior in neurological terms may be in a habit formation, and that habit pattern is very difficult to break. I would suggest that the most common manifestation of a neurological pattern is a language pattern where a person might have been making statements to themselves for so long, along the lines that "I'm not worthy, I don't have any real value," that the habit is not even noticeable. This language pattern is held in the limbic system—the literal part of the brain where the autonomic body functions operate from. It is where our breathing and other body functions operate and receive their direction from. Every time you say "I'm not worthy," that part of the brain takes it literally that you are not worthy. It gets the story that you have no worth.

The story can then become its perpetual wounding. If one tells a story about themselves and possibly it is the one-hundredth time of telling that same story, it is then so deeply embedded in the individual that it has become neurologically patterned or embedded into their existence. Breaking the habit of that story requires a very conscious effort. That pattern is one that cannot be broken energetically, per se. It requires that you consciously go in and break the pattern yourself. As mentioned earlier, this becomes a choice to deal with it consciously, if the person wants to be well.

What happens with this Mordrigal energy is that it comes in, and, again, it is like an electrical short-circuit. If an individual has ever gone to the electrical circuit breaker box in their home because the power went out in some part of their home, they try to turn it on, and it goes right back off. This is what Mordrigal is doing on the surface of one's body. This energy is cutting off the connections provided by the chakras between the physical and spiritual planes. Reference chapter 3 for a detailed description of how chakras function.

What happens when this new protocol emerges is there is a very specific pattern to the chakra that presents itself, which to me, indicates the presence of Mordrigal. I suspect that individual healers may see the presence in different ways than I see it, and that is certainly okay. However, by my observation, the presentation is always the same, and I think for those who have participated in the training, frequently, the presenting pattern is similar.

I will now present the protocol in very specific steps so that both the client and the practitioner can have a basic concept of the procedure. When training in this area, the actual class covers approximately sixty hours of time and much work with putting these processes into muscle memory for the practitioner. The context here is placed within the carefully designed treatment setting. There are numerous tools and techniques for the shamanic practitioner to maximize their levels of protection. Examples include the use of Vogel crystals for extraction, possibly crystal-powered wands, wearing dark clothing not to be seen as readily, and so on.

The "Mordrigal Protocol" is as follows:

1. The single most important part of the protocol is to create a safe, protected environment for the interventions to take place. It is very important NOT to take these interventions casually. These treatments require consistency and persistence. It is also of utmost importance for the individual practitioner to practice a very high degree of spiritual hygiene. Every tradition or mystery school, hopefully, has a protocol of preparation for the practitioner to bring themselves into a level of preparation to enter another realm. Here it is to safeguard the treatment setting by setting up essentially impenetrable boundaries. The same goes for the practitioner to set up those boundaries of impenetrability within themselves. The techniques are numerous though essentially are common sense. The single most important concept is to take the intervention strategies delineated here very seriously and utilize great care in protecting oneself.

2. Open sacred space by calling out to the four directions, the Pachamama (Mother Earth), and the Great Spirit in whatever words, phrases, and thoughts are meaningful to you.

3. When reading the chakras as described previously, a unique pattern presents itself. The first time going over

all seven chakras with the pendulum, in a manner that holds the energy of the client, the first pass has all seven chakras going in a clockwise spinning direction. The second time going over all seven chakras, the pendulum is rotating counterclockwise. The third pass over all seven chakras, each one is closed, reflected as no movement whatsoever of the pendulum. This pattern then repeats itself over and over. The fourth time the pendulum is going clockwise over all seven chakras. The fifth time the pendulum is going counterclockwise. The sixth time they are closed. The seventh, eighth, and ninth times the same. This repeats and repeats, indicating that the energetic form of Mordrigal is in play. It has short-circuited the chakra system so that the individual is not connected to their higher self, their luminous field, their Song of the Soul. This begins to provide some understanding of the phenomenon of isolation as a defining characteristic of the Mordrigal energetic form. Why the individual may feel lost. They are no longer connected on any level, with not even any potential to hear the Song of the Soul. It has been hijacked, interrupted by Mordrigal. Remember, though, the Song of the Soul has not gone anywhere. It is alive and well, waiting for the individual to be once again able to tune in! This is the first step of the intervention, to read the chakras and realize that there is an overlay of this energetic form called Mordrigal. This intervention and initial assessment can be done remotely by having the client blow their energy into something being held to the earpiece of the practitioner and the client blowing their energy into the mouthpiece of their phone. Then, all the same procedures endure for that client, just the same as if they were present in the treatment room. It does work, even if this may be entirely unfamiliar to the reader.

4. The next step is to remove the overlay by sweeping the energetic field with an extraction crystal numerous times (four to five times). Safely, either clear the crystal or place it in a position to withstand any further interference from this energetic form. Out of habit, I tend to place it in a significant position, like at an open window with the clear intention that Mordrigal may not reenter the treatment area or room. It is beneficial to stress here that one is not finished with this part of the intervention protocol until they are completely satisfied the energetic form has been successfully removed. In other words, each stage of intervention requires consistent and repeated measurement that the energy has been displaced from the client. Success in removal of the overlay is revealed by seeing a more typical pattern of chakra behavior, repeatedly presenting the same pattern, which then assures that the client's chakras are being perceived rather than the energy of Mordrigal. The overlay has been removed successfully.

5. Then it is to look for the centers that appear to hold control of the situation. As mentioned previously in chapter 4, the physician drew me to the base of the neck as the center for control. Here the practitioner asks the client to turn over onto their stomach and begins the extraction to remove the energy centered at that location. It is required to have a sensitive tracking ability to know where and the degree of the energy being held and to extract until the energy is no longer there. This involves

the shamanic practitioner's tool bag for the methods they use to accomplish the removal of energies such as this. In my case, I utilize what I refer to as a cutting tool, however, it would appear much more like a scraper that would not be able to cut anything, much less harm my client. I show the client exactly what I am using if we are working in person. Remotely, I am working on top of a cloth that reflects the seven chakras and, at this point, working directly over the backside of the fifth chakra. Simultaneously, I am also holding an extraction crystal in my other hand to capture the energy that is being released.

6.   The same process then occurs at the base of the spine if there is energy also located there.

Following the backside intervention, then ask the client to turn onto their backside and proceed with the removal of the foreign energy at the first root chakra if it is there, and very specifically at the throat chakra. The throat chakra is the key to successfully removing these controlling energies. I think of these controlling centers as some type of sending and/or receiving units, as defined previously.

7.   At this point, it is important to check again that you have been successful in removing all evidence of the energetic form of Mordrigal, from the client's external body surface. If there is a sense that any of these energies continue to exist, or perhaps return while you are working, go back until you have successfully removed the energetic form. I have found that on occasion, the overlay will return during the session, so I never think

it is too often or too many times to check, both with the pendulum and my tracking stone in my hand to feel for the energy located at the fifth and sometimes first chakras.

8. Then proceed with the session as you would always conduct it, whatever that may look like. It is important to know that there remains work to be done in extracting Mordrigal from the underworld as well, however, it is seemingly not appropriate to go into this in-depth in this context. It is to rely on the training and competence of the practitioner first to remove the Mordrigal energetic form as it exists in the underworld, and then to proceed in the search for the fractures in the soul where this energy finds its entry. This is work that is specific to in-depth training for the advanced shamanic practitioner.

I propose, as I have delineated in this Mordrigal Protocol, that it is not a difficult intervention. It is one that requires wisdom. It requires looking with eyes wide open! It is quick in its application, once the practitioner gains comfort with the protocol. My experience is that this can often be accomplished within roughly fifteen minutes or less. That is what is meant by referring to this protocol as a simple protocol, yet in reality, there is very little that is simple about it. This protocol is effective when properly applied.

Once I had begun teaching around this process, the students were able to further evolve the protocol by identifying that a similar control center could be located at the first chakra as well as at the fifth. When it has been stated that this is an evolving protocol, I invite further exploration and further evolution of this protocol. What is presented here is offered with that understanding. There remains more to be understood and evolved within this frame of reference.

The Mordrigal energetic form can manifest in the first chakra. When it involves the root chakra, it can create sensations that are not always good, however, sensations that can sometimes also be enticing are created as well. The Mordrigal energetic form is a trickster. It is clever and hides very effectively. That is where the true seer comes in. Once one knows what to look for, the potential to be tricked into not seeing it decreases significantly.

In a like manner for the client, once again, it is to remind one that the process is a matter of increasing one's awareness of the separation between having the energetic form of Mordrigal upon and within them and knowing the difference when that form has been removed. It is the process of traveling from being unaware to gaining the awareness of what it feels like to be free of it. It is to know that the Mordrigal energetic form is not the same as the individual; indeed, it is quite separate. When the talk of worthlessness and shame enters, manifesting as loneliness and isolation, they are the talking points of the Mordrigal energetic form and not the individual.

Going forth, this is the protocol. This hopefully opens up the door. Once these manifestations of Mordrigal are removed, the practitioner can then go into a session where one can go and travel into the underworld and do the necessary and important work of healing. It is in the underworld where we find the fractures, the wounds that have been written about, and where healing has to take place. Again, this falls into the domain of the trained shaman, the journeyer, the one who can make the journeys into these other realms and work there as well.

In summary, this intervention protocol is not difficult to realize. I would not be writing about it if I thought it was something majestically difficult. I would keep it secret. What it requires is the ability to open one's eyes, if you're a practitioner, and see it for what it is. The same applies to the client. Deal honestly with the reality that, "Hey, this is a pattern I have not seen before. This is a pattern that seems odd, and it seems unusual." I invite you to start looking at it within the eyes of a protocol, and I wish to state to the tune of all the sessions I have referred to, it works. It unequivocally works. Depending on how long a person has been suffering from this, the Mordrigal energetic form can be back within thirty seconds, in three hours, three days, or not at all. The single most frustrating and infuriating aspect of Mordrigal is the persistence with which it violates its victims. It is the same persistence that is required in the treatment of this sickness.

This is a protocol of awareness. It is necessary to have an awareness and then an openness to see it, not to be frightened of it. Fear prevents one from seeing. Fear is one of the biggest issues blocking the energy of anything. If an individual is terrified of something, it energizes it. Regarding "fear" and working with or experiencing this energetic form, fear is like feeding Mordrigal dinner at the Golden Buffet. Fear on special, dinner served.

CHAPTER 8

THE EMPOWERMENT
OF SOUL

The action of walking in nonjudgment may be one of the hardest steps anyone can take. That does not mean to ignore or forgive egregious behavior that is occurring right in front of one's eyes. It means to be capable of immediate action as necessary and then hold the ability also to look past and find the forgiveness embedded in healing. There are battles to be fought that will free one from their fears and limitations to become the architect of his or her own life.

The writing in this book has traveled through a great deal of territory, beginning with a newly minted concept of the luminous energy field holding the Song of the Soul. This is one of the ways we can view and connect to our higher selves. There is the definition of shamanism, the shamanic practitioner, and briefly the shamanic warrior. A dark energetic form and the naming of it as Mordrigal is found in chapter 4.

The concept of soul fractures is introduced as a potential turning point in our ability to absorb and understand the gravity of violence in all forms, and the devastation that results from it. It is here in the long-term consequences of violence where the healing at the deepest energetic level is required and necessary. Finally, a protocol for healing from the dark was introduced, and now resources for realizing new maps to wholeness are offered.

Referring again to Nancy Portland, she has been one of the more severe situations encountered. Over four years with treatment throughout, she shared her more recent thoughts regarding this energetic form of Mordrigal.

> For the record, there was one night where I felt as though a cattle prod was being used to paralyze and

bring excruciating pain to my legs, from my hips down focused particularly in the calf of each leg. What's the point of this? This is what floats its boat, misery? To make you so miserable that you will kill yourself?

When she was studying for an advanced degree in social work, Nancy reflected that in the entire MA program for clinical social work in her experience, maybe one class at the most was devoted to suicide phenomena. Via her initiative, she studied suicide in-depth for about six months. A researcher named Edwin Schneidman, in a book entitled *The Suicide Mind*, studied suicide notes from several police department files and came up with one four-letter word as most predictive of suicide. That word is only, meaning "to pause." He went on to state that it is urgent to widen the perspective of the individual as quickly as possible. The semicolon is becoming the universal symbol of suicide prevention leading to the idea of giving notice or emphasizing the concept to "pause" if you are considering suicide as the "only" option available. In a certain sense, the writing on these pages ultimately surrounds the near epidemic phenomenon of suicide. The essential goal in this writing is to give notice to pause, that there is hope for those who find themselves stuck in the quagmire of suicidal ideology.

When Nancy woke up the next morning, she realized that something else has greater power over her, whether it is her celestial parents or otherwise. This thing, the energetic form of Mordrigal, when attacking tells its victim that this is the only way. This energetic form creates misery, which leads to fear and then to self-destruction. There is help, and there are alternatives!

This energetic form, [this Mordrigal] had convinced me that I would hurt either my partner or my dog. Upon awakening the next day, I realized that this energy no longer has power over me. Stupid because it is so basic! The fact is that it does what it does with a very sophisticated form of technology. My shaman can see it on a person, but what is it? It is something that is sophisticated in a way that we are not prepared for! It is so repetitive saying or implying to its victims 'You're doomed, you're going to die!' Truth is that we don't know the technology that is attacking us. Are there all these kinds of beings around us, or is it the same energy? Stupid, stupid, stupid! Yet four years, and how can I say stupid? In the year 2017, I was convinced to such a degree that I took an overdose. This is something way beyond…

Can an individual ever be happy again? Is that a question that might be asked if one has experienced the energetic form of Mordrigal? Is it possible to be happy, to know oneself again? Will an individual ever find their Song of the Soul? The answer is yes, individuals can and will find for themselves their Song of the Soul and reconnect with their higher self.

You might be wondering what happens when this energy is removed. Immediately, an individual might simply feel different, though many clients have reported feeling much more hopeful. The feeling of happiness coming back into their lives. Suicidal thoughts lessened or disappeared completely. Yet, the data here also notice the victims of this energetic form must proceed with a certain degree of caution as well.

A metaphor worth considering is what happens in the event of an earthquake. It is violent and destructive and occurs within a moment, often without a moment's notice. Destructive, yet some things remain intact. It is the tremors that follow that are chilling to the bone if one has survived. There are tremors all over the place with broken relationships, jobs, homes, communities. The tremors bring it all back, terrorizing the victims again and again. The earthquake is the soul fracture, the destruction is Mordrigal, while the tremors are the long-lasting remnants that reside in the body's memory. Someone close reflected how walking over one of the grates that ventilate the subway systems in Chicago brought back immediately the visceral memory of surviving the earthquake in Oakland, California, in 1989.

When the healing comes into fruition, the traumas, the fractures become pieces of data that no longer hold the tears and anxiety of the soul. Instead, they are remembered as information. Those items did not go away, but now, they are more in the category of data and information. The traumas or fractures are no longer the stories that have to be told fifty more times. They are done; now, information and life can go on without the same degree of pain being present.

Walking within freedom is to walk in a healed state. The journey to walking in freedom can also be one of the most terrorizing experiences. When an individual finds their way to being freed from Mordrigal, it is a huge leap forward. It is the bells of freedom ringing loud and clear, and the person's Song of the Soul only gets louder and louder. It is coming in stronger, minute by minute.

A question very frequently asked is, how do I keep this energy off of me? How do I stay clear? How do I not get attacked again? To answer that question, I want to go back to Simone Weil, who has been referenced earlier in this book, and her discussions around affliction and the miserableness that is created by this dark energy force. While she does not put forth a protocol in the same way as in this book, at least a somewhat parallel term that she uses is metaxu. In very simplistic terms, metaxu is building bridges back to life. Building bridges back into the Song of the Soul. Building bridges and finding gateways that take one back into the life once known, before moving toward isolation.

The expression of metaxu is manifested in the building blocks of reuniting the individual with his or her life. It is rebuilding relationships with children, partners, and spouses. Building relations with extended family that have deteriorated during this time, because during the time of healing, boundaries had to be set. It is a beginning. It is that process of how you go back into the world and still hold healthy boundaries, yet find your way back in. Simone Weil, one hundred years ago, was writing about bridging people back into their lives.

Recently Ms. Sharp contacted me again for additional work around the Mordrigal issue. It had been fourteen months since we last worked together. Ms. Sharp was devastated by the fact that some days earlier, the energetic form of Mordrigal had reentered her being and was bringing forth many of the same symptoms that had been worked with earlier. I was greatly relieved to understand that the attack had happened some nine days earlier, important because she did not fall into the trap of isolating herself in despair. It is important to confess here, to potential clients, to those experiencing this Mordrigal energetic form, that yes, this unwanted, unwelcome energy can and may return with a vengeance, not unlike the tremor that brings back the less than desirable visceral memories associated with surviving an earthquake.

If there is some type of vaccination that occurs, it is that once freed from the Mordrigal energetic form, one knows exactly what it is and no longer has to go through that initial process of wondering what is wrong or going on. The work with her was rapid and effective. In a certain sense, we are picking up where we left off, and she appears to be ready to take the next steps in her healing journey. She describes the past fourteen-month period as being positive and full of a robust reconnection with her soul, and especially her relationship with her two children.

Sweet Melissa experienced huge leaps of progress in reentering into her family and extended family structure. For the first time, she was excited to be home over the holidays with her family. There remain major hurdles ahead for her. We discovered in a very recent session that during the crucial developmental years, when she started drinking at the age of eleven, she missed very important learning about social interactions. Sweet Melissa has major goals in front of her that will challenge her to continue reaching for and into her higher self. She has already demonstrated that she is more than capable of doing this. She notes that it is now to figure out the rest of her life.

One clear measure of progress is the measure of integration, the reverse side of isolation. In the situation for Ms. Sharp, she was diagnosed as being floridly psychotic. Yet, she knew she was not truly in such a state. Her journey to once again connecting with her children, writing a new book, and gradually reentering

her academic life, reflects the profound journey of returning to
one's passion in life. Nancy Portland returns to finding her way
back to her life's passion in the arts and living robustly within
her community. These stories attest to the power of healing.
Those are the measures that reflect the treatment, the success.

This information is shared here with only full heart, soul,
and honesty. Transcending toward the higher forms of
consciousness related to power is a matter of facing one's
fears and unresolved issues that can carry immense amounts
of toxic energy. The worst-case scenarios are reflected in the
presence, the entry of the energetic form of Mordrigal. It is
now to remind all readers that once this energetic form is
released, with the use of the protocol or otherwise, it is then
that the healing interventions can take place, providing for
the deepest of healing. Such treatment requires persistence
and consistency in breaking long-standing patterns related to
an individual's beliefs and behaviors.

When the healing comes into fruition, the traumas—the
fractures—become pieces of data that no longer hold the soul
in their vice-grips. Instead, the soul is brought back together
into wholeness. Those stories now become information while
life can then go on without so much pain being present. The
thrill of walking with freedom is to walk in a healed state. It is
to recognize here that the journey to walking in freedom can
be one of the hardest things an individual will ever do. It can
be terrorizing, yet the reward, the thrill when one can find this
freedom, is enormous. It is the bells of freedom ringing loud
and clear, and the person's Song of the Soul only gets louder
and stronger.

I have been referring to the Song of the Soul as the connection to building relationships again within an individual's world. This is very critical. Rebuilding relationships with children, partners, spouses, and extended family are of major importance in countering the isolation of Mordrigal. During the healing of these deepest wounds, boundaries have to be set. That is the beginning place for the healing, particularly as it pertains to shame. That is how one goes back into his or her world and can still manage to hold healthy boundaries. It is a learning process, and one is never too old to learn.

The awareness, the knowledge is that an individual's Sacred Shield creates a type of defense, an immunization. When an individual knows what this energetic form is, one can choose to step through it and do the healing work that is needed, as well as hold the knowledge to protect oneself from it. An individual is then no longer as susceptible to the Mordrigal energetic form. It becomes much more difficult for such energies to isolate an individual, break his or her back, cause one to kill themselves. Individuals can now walk with awareness, walking back in the world that is known. Once again, an individual can listen to their Song of the Soul and raise their protective shield.

There are ways of maintaining the healed state and invoking protections. An individual can request or "invoke high-frequency support." One can engage, create, and build their own Sacred Shield. It is a matter of finding essentially the powers that exist within an individual's world. Use imagination. Individuals are permitted to be coated in violet armor if they choose. What are the qualities desired? Create a certain construction that cleanses. Understand one's vulnerabilities and construct the shield accordingly, using alchemy to transmute any energies an individual wishes to change. Pick from this list and add others that are known, desired, or imagined. There are no limits!

A menu of some high-frequency supports:

- Fire ceremony
- Sacred geometry
- Creating an altar to anchor energy
- Crystals
- Crystal wands
- Your outfit—black is harder to see
- Christ consciousness
- Archangels
- Meditation
- Sacred Space
- Animal totems
- Singing bowls
- Sound healing
- Music
- Special to you: _____

The individual's Sacred Shield is raised when going into battle. Having been victimized by an attempted kidnapping in a foreign country recently, while sitting in the back of a car that I should not have been in, being taken down the road and realizing my life was in danger, I raised my Sacred Shield. Quickly, I was able to make it very clear that I was not going to have it.

My Sacred Shield came up automatically as I have engaged in a considerable amount of healing work on myself. I made a choice many years ago to be well. To do the things necessary to be well, to find the healing set. Everyone can make that choice, to become healed, to become strong, to pick up one's Sacred Shield. I am not going to play with somebody trying to kidnap me, somebody trying to extort me, perhaps even trying to kill me, ultimately. I am not going to have it. It is not in the range of options. Not possible.

An individual can make a choice, to step in against the bullies of the world, to assist the people suffering and challenged to find their way. If we call shame out for what it is, then others will begin to think and understand shame in a way that it can be healed more forthrightly. These concepts help to create one's Sacred Shield. An individual's Sacred Shield is in the heart. How does one want to be in this world? How does one want to carry themselves? If an individual does their work and works from and with their heart, they are moving in a profoundly powerful direction. The ability to create one's Sacred Shield has been there all along. It is to seize it and raise it high and mightily. The universe responds to people who take action. The universe responds to people who help themselves. The universe responds to people who set clear intentions. The universe is listening, and you will receive confirmation. Embrace the Song of Your Soul!

CREATE, BUILD, AND
RAISE YOUR OWN SACRED SHIELD!

THE TIME IS NOW.

AFTERWORD

Sometimes it is just to stop fighting—let go and open your heart. This is winning the battle because the strength of love is the source of all life and our greatest protection. This is now a call to action! This is now an invitation to join in the healing of our human collective. With the Sacred Shield at hand, it is possible for everyone to find in his or her own heart, the heart of each, the compassion of unconditional love.

A major difference that has occurred over the last 100 years since Simone Weil wrote about metaxu, may be the complexity and intrigue of society reflected in the digital media traps, the vast access to medicinal opioids, the easy availability of guns, and the profound polarization being realized universally. Shame is playing throughout in the form of top-level secrets being held by those attempting to realize absolute power. Lying and hiding information may well be a function of covering up shame. The advent of fake news, of institutional lying could well be a function of suffering under the effects of the Mordrigal energetic form. Utilizing force is a methodology that rings from dishonesty and manipulation. Force resides with the levels of consciousness associated with shame, guilt, fear, anger and pride. These are all opportunities to realize negative outcomes. These types of outcomes can open the door to increasing the phenomenon of isolation and the energetic forms of Mordrigal, wetiko, malignant egophrenia, or affliction as dark energetic forms capable of impacting every human being on the planet. The other side of force rests power as defined by acceptance, reason, love, joy and peace (Hawkins, *Power vs. Force*).

Within this paradigm, considering the free reign that the dark energetic form of Mordrigal has had, are there correlations to today's various realities? Do the opioid crisis and the very high degree of deaths associated have anything to do with this energetic form or some other similar energetic form? This book has been talking about a tear or fracture in one's energetic field where the soul resides. This is where this very dark energy form enters. Is there a fracture in our greater community, our global community where we can see political fractures, environmental fractures, racial fractures, isolation, and extreme income inequality? These are questions for all of us to ponder as we proceed with our directions in life.

If one is open to assessment, it is to know and understand the presence and the degree to which these types of energetic forms exist in the energetic world today. It is also to begin to understand the toll that energetic forms such as those presented here are extracting from all of us in one way or another. This writing has been generated entirely from the heart, the soul, and the extraordinary realities presented by the many clients, students, and colleagues throughout these many years of practice. I might add, that as I was training, the very earliest realization for me was that I was remembering, as opposed to learning the shamanic way from scratch. The remembering generated a great deal of this information. Thank you for journeying along with me here and thank you, Spirit, for allowing us to sing the Song of Life together, one more day. PWB

APPENDIX

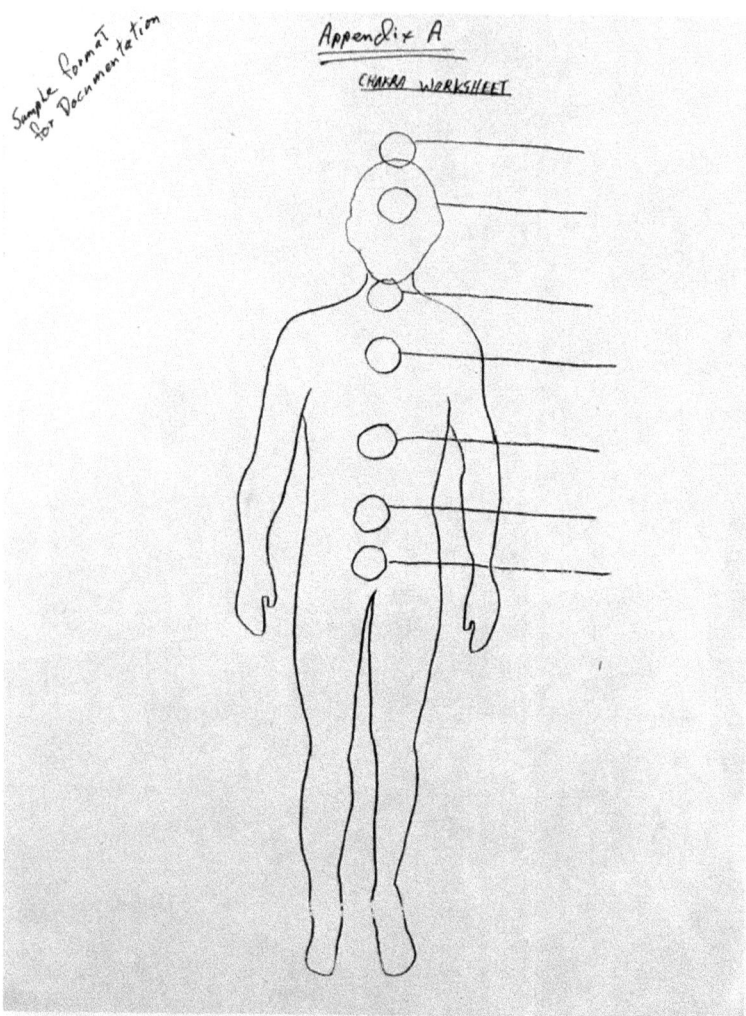

Appendix A: Sample of one-page data collection form, over
1,300 utilized as the baseline data for this book.

Appendix B

CHAKRA WORKSHEET

Name: Samples of Completed Format

Date: 3/21/10 Time: 3:00pm

Energetic Clearing Contract experienced from violent perpetrator (Trauma @ age 24 (Client Now in 50's)

at beginning of removal of strange hold on clients neck

Illumination
G9
Journey to chamber of contracts to remove, curse against perpetrator's daughter

removal of crystallized energy around neck

Illum
De-Couple

Soul Retrieval
- Flower Dress young woman
- Kite as gift
- Jaguar as power animal

- Much Preparation for clearing including pictures of environment.

- Worked first on Client's neck where violent item was held against her.

- Set up office to emulate environment due to remote nature of this effort (by phone across continents)

Clearing began with determining center as being on the Veranda - Then proceeded to the outside all the way to the perimeter entry point where the lack of safety was most disarming.
- The most severe area was behind a Salvaged entry door blocking a bunch of unknown items in the garage.

Total Time: 3 Hours

→ When clearing was complete, then an individual healing session took place to work on the remnants physically and Spiritually being held within the energetic field.

Appendix B: Sample of an actual completed data collection form, reflecting the intake information on the left side and the actions taken at the top right side. Also reflects any physical issues dealt with on the physical body.

RESOURCE/REFERENCE

1. Arvay, Clemens G. (2018). *The Biophilia Effect: A Scientific and Spiritual Exploration of the Healing Bond Between Humans and Nature.* (Ruediger Dahlke, Trans.). Boulder, Colorado: Sounds True.

2. Clifford, M. Amnos (2018). *Your Guide to Forest Bathing: Experience the Healing Power of Nature.* Newburyport, MA: Conari Press.

3. Emoto, Masaru (2004). *The Hidden Messages in Water.* (David A. Thayne, Trans.). Hillsboro, Oregon: Beyond Words Publishing, Inc.

4. Forbes, Jack D. (2008). *Columbus and Other Cannibals.* (Rev. Ed.). New York, NY: Seven Stories Press.

5. Harner, Michael (2013). *Cave and Cosmos: Shamanic Encounters with Another Reality.* Berkeley, CA: North Atlantic Books.

6. Hawkins, David (2013). *Power vs. Force: The Hidden Determinants of Human Behavior.* Carlsbad, CA: Hay House.

7. Nerburn, Kent (Ed.). *The Wisdom of the Native Americans.* Novato, CA: New World Library.

8. Levy, Paul (2013). *Dispelling Wetiko: Breaking the Curse of Evil.* Berkeley, CA: North Atlantic Books.

9. Panichas, George A. (Ed.) (1977). *The Simone Weil Reader.* Wakefield, Rhode Island and London: Moyer Bell

10. Shlain, Leonard (1998). *The Alphabet Versus The Goddess: the Conflict Between Word and Image.* New York, NY: Penquin / Compass.

11. Villoldo, Alberto (2000). *Shaman, Healer, Sage: How to Heal Yourself and Others with the Energy Medicine of the Americas.* New York, NY: Harmony Books.

INDEX

SACRED SHIELD

and fear, 72
importance of nonjudging in, 120, 144
ingredients of, 35
as needed for things that happen in the energetic world, 69
remotely, 55–56, 126, 136–137
timing of, 9, 34
typical beginning for sessions, 126–128
use of circular time with, 45
use of dark clothing by shamanic practitioner, 135, 152
with victims of sexual violence, 97
shamanic journeying, 45, 46
shamanic warrior, 56–58, 77
shamanism
described, 34
history of, 12
lineages of, 23, 51, 54
as practice and not religion, 34, 46
as pulling information from natural world, 18
shame
bullying and, 97–101
characteristics of, 86
consequences of feeling, 96
described, 93
externalization of, 107
function of, 101
hesitancy to discuss, 93–94
infliction of, 14
as inner dialogue, 9
internalization of, 107
as invitation to dark energy, 67–68
process of getting through, 102
seeing of energetically, 97
and suicide, 97
shape-shifting, 78
Shapiro, Francine, 102
Sharp, Ms., as case example, 103, 104, 121–123, 148
Shinrin-Yoku (forest bathing), 21–22
singing bowls
as high-frequency support, 152
use of, 26
sleep loss, Mordrigal energy and, 10, 77
somatic memory work, 102
Song of the Soul
ability to hear, 24
as collective, 24
as constant, 25
defined, xiv, 20–21
emotions as expression/voice of, 24
existence of, 19, 24
as having no negative, 28
hijacking of, 63–64
losing touch with, 27–28
as metaphor, xiv, 19, 20, 116
Mordrigal as interrupting ability to hear, 68, 78
as not having dialogue, 25
presence of in all sentient beings, 21, 22–23
as residing in luminous body, 39

as ultimate protection, 23
as unique to each person, 19, 21
use of term, 18
"Song of the Soul" (song), 18, 29
soul
bright light of, 12
dark night of, 12
homing device of, 47–48
light of, 21
remembering parts of, 46–47
splintering/tearing of, 7
soul fracture
as almost always involved boundary violations, 105
bullying and, 106
causes of, 70–71, 97
defined, 91
earthquake as metaphor for, 147
manifestation of, 101
use of term, xv, 9, 24, 97, 144
where it lives, 128
soul retrieval, 33, 46–47
sound
as auditory technology, 26
communications of in forests, 21–22
healing aspects of, 19–20, 21
importance of, 26–27
use of in world of energy, 18
sound healing, as high-frequency support, 152
Spirit, contract of with shaman, 49
spiritual hygiene, as practiced by shamanic practitioner, 135
spirituality, shamanism as oldest form of, 12
St. Peter's Cathedral (Rome), as evidence of lost technologies, 26
suicidal thoughts/suicidal ideation, 3, 4, 67, 68, 87, 89–90, 91, 145, 146
suicide, as near epidemic phenomenon, 145
The Suicide Mind (Schneidman), 145
Sun Empire, 23, 25–26, 51
Sweet Melissa, as case example, 86–91, 92, 129–130, 131–132, 133, 149
symbols, power in, 50–51
synchronicity, 48–49

T

technologies, evidence of ones that have been lost, 25–26
terpenes, 21, 22
third eye, 41
throat chakra, importance of, 138
tics, 10, 133
time dimensions, 45–46
tracking stone, use of, 139
trauma, potential impact of severe trauma, 9–10, 11–12, 14. See also sexual abuse/trauma/molestation/violation/violence
true self, 10
truth, 44–45